THE SOCIOECONOMIC EFFECTS OF PUBLIC SECTOR INFORMATION ON DIGITAL NETWORKS
TOWARD A BETTER UNDERSTANDING OF DIFFERENT ACCESS AND REUSE POLICIES

WORKSHOP SUMMARY

Paul F. Uhlir, Rapporteur

U.S. National Committee for CODATA
Board on Research Data and Information
Policy and Global Affairs

in collaboration with the
Working Party on the Information Economy
Organisation for Economic Co-operation and Development

NATIONAL RESEARCH COUNCIL
OF THE NATIONAL ACADEMIES

THE NATIONAL ACADEMIES PRESS
Washington, D.C.
www.nap.edu

THE NATIONAL ACADEMIES PRESS 500 Fifth Street, N.W. Washington, DC 20001

NOTICE: The project that is the subject of this report was approved by the Governing Board of the National Research Council, whose members are drawn from the councils of the National Academy of Sciences, the National Academy of Engineering, and the Institute of Medicine. The members of the committee responsible for the report were chosen for their special competences and with regard for appropriate balance.

This study was supported by the National Science Foundation under Grant No. GEO-0738128 and by the United States Geological Service under Grant No. 07HQGR0177. Any opinions, findings, conclusions, or recommendations expressed in this publication are those of the author(s) and do not necessarily reflect the views of the organizations or agencies that provided support for the project.

International Standard Book Number 13: 978-0-309-13968-7
International Standard Book Number 10: 0-309-13968-6

Additional copies of this report are available from the National Academies Press, 500 Fifth Street, N.W., Lockbox 285, Washington, DC 20055; (800) 624-6242 or (202) 334-3313 (in the Washington metropolitan area); Internet, *http://www.nap.edu*.

Copyright 2009 by the National Academy of Sciences. All rights reserved.

Printed in the United States of America

THE NATIONAL ACADEMIES
Advisers to the Nation on Science, Engineering, and Medicine

The **National Academy of Sciences** is a private, nonprofit, self-perpetuating society of distinguished scholars engaged in scientific and engineering research, dedicated to the furtherance of science and technology and to their use for the general welfare. Upon the authority of the charter granted to it by the Congress in 1863, the Academy has a mandate that requires it to advise the federal government on scientific and technical matters. Dr. Ralph J. Cicerone is president of the National Academy of Sciences.

The **National Academy of Engineering** was established in 1964, under the charter of the National Academy of Sciences, as a parallel organization of outstanding engineers. It is autonomous in its administration and in the selection of its members, sharing with the National Academy of Sciences the responsibility for advising the federal government. The National Academy of Engineering also sponsors engineering programs aimed at meeting national needs, encourages education and research, and recognizes the superior achievements of engineers. Dr. Charles M. Vest is president of the National Academy of Engineering.

The **Institute of Medicine** was established in 1970 by the National Academy of Sciences to secure the services of eminent members of appropriate professions in the examination of policy matters pertaining to the health of the public. The Institute acts under the responsibility given to the National Academy of Sciences by its congressional charter to be an adviser to the federal government and, upon its own initiative, to identify issues of medical care, research, and education. Dr. Harvey V. Fineberg is president of the Institute of Medicine.

The **National Research Council** was organized by the National Academy of Sciences in 1916 to associate the broad community of science and technology with the Academy's purposes of furthering knowledge and advising the federal government. Functioning in accordance with general policies determined by the Academy, the Council has become the principal operating agency of both the National Academy of Sciences and the National Academy of Engineering in providing services to the government, the public, and the scientific and engineering communities. The Council is administered jointly by both Academies and the Institute of Medicine. Dr. Ralph J. Cicerone and Dr. Charles M. Vest are chair and vice chair, respectively, of the National Research Council.

www.national-academies.org

STEERING COMMITTEE ON THE SOCIOECONOMIC EFFECTS OF PUBLIC SECTOR INFORMATION ON DIGITAL NETWORKS

Roberta Balstad *(Chair)*, Columbia University

Christine Borgman, University of California, Los Angeles

John Houghton, Victoria University, Australia

Harlan Onsrud, University of Maine

Knut Rexed, Rexed & Spröndly, DB, Sweden

U.S. NATIONAL COMMITTEE FOR CODATA
(as of February 2008)

Roberta Balstad *(Chair)*, Columbia University

Bonnie Carroll, Information International Associates
Hal Abelson, Massachusetts Institute of Technology
Peter Arzberger, University of California, San Diego
Helen M. Berman, Rutgers University
Christine Borgman, University of California, Los Angeles
Sara Graves, University of Alabama
Myron Gutmann, Inter-University Consortium for Political and Social Research
Krishna Rajan, Iowa State University
David Scott, Rice University
Mary Waltham, Publishing Consultant

Working Party on the Information Economy (WPIE)[1]

Daniela Battisti *(Chair ad interim)*, Italy

Josie Brocca *(Vice Chair)*, Canada
Antti Eskola *(Vice Chair)*, Finland
Sangwon Ko *(Vice Chair)*, Korea
Doreen McGirr *(Vice Chair)*, United States

Egypt (Regular Observer)
Russian Federation (Regular Observer)
Estonia (Regular Observer)
Singapore (Regular Observer)
India (Regular Observer)
South Africa (Regular Observer)
Israel (Regular Observer)

---

[1] WPIE membership is open to all thirty member states of the OECD; regular observers are not currently member states.

Preface

Governments are the compilers and owners of a great deal of digital information, from geospatial data to statistical compilations and real estate records. In particular, the member countries of the Organisation for Economic Co-operation and Development (OECD) have made huge investments in generating and disseminating public sector information (PSI), in large part because of the recognition that there are very significant socioeconomic values of and effects from this information. This is recognized to be especially true for PSI on the Internet. Unfortunately, however, there is relatively little empirical data available on the effects of PSI disseminated online or on the various policy approaches that are now being taken to this dissemination, and what data that do exist are generally neither detailed nor comprehensive. This state of affairs leaves policy makers and information managers without the facts they need to assess and improve these policies. Thus there is a clear and compelling need to better understand what the large public investment in the creation of public sector information can produce or is already producing.

Because of the important potential economic and social benefits of PSI activities in the United States and in other OECD countries, the U.S. National Committee for CODATA[1] and the OECD organized an international workshop on February 4-5, 2008, aimed at obtaining an improved understanding of the methods, models, and techniques used to assess the specific effects of different access and reuse policies for PSI disseminated online. Specifically, the workshop was designed to address the following questions:

1. Why is a better understanding of the specific economic and non-economic values and effects of policies of access to and reuse[2] of PSI important? What could be done to improve knowledge of these issues?

2. What is the state of the art in different approaches for evaluating the direct and indirect economic and non-economic benefits and costs of access and reuse policies for PSI in the online environment? Define the underlying concepts and survey the literature about these policies and assessment methods.

3. How have these methods been applied, for what types of information, and by which organizations? What are the commonalities and differences among the various methods in relation to the types of information and policies being assessed?

---

[1] CODATA is the Committee on Data for Science and Technology, an interdisciplinary body of the International Council for Science in Paris. The mission of CODATA is to strengthen international science for the benefit of society by promoting improved scientific and technical data management and use. See, http://www.codata.org/. The U.S. National Committee for CODATA has been the U.S. national member in CODATA at the National Academy of Sciences for more than three decades.

[2] According to the OECD report, *Digital Broadband Content: Public Sector Information and Content,* 2006. Working Party on the Information Economy. DSTI/ICCP. Paris: OECD, "reuse" is focused on exploiting the economic value of public information (p.10). There are also many other cases, however, in which end users only "use" this information for their own purposes, such as personal education and other socially focused activities without adding any value to the original PSI. Because reuse potentially involves much broader and greater economic (as well as non-economic) effects, the workshop focused primarily on the reuse of PSI and distinguished between reuse and end use only where that distinction was important.

4. What are the criteria to assess the validity and reliability of such methods? What is known or still needs to be known about the application of these methods to the evaluation of public information policies in the online environment?

5. Identify a range of best practices, theoretical frameworks, and models that are currently used to assess the economic and non-economic value and effects of different policies of access to and reuse of digital PSI,

6. Identify a range of activities that might be undertaken by information managers and policy makers in the OECD countries to enhance understanding of the economic and non-economic value and effects of different policies of access to and reuse of digital PSI.

The first day and a half of the workshop were focused on tasks 1-4, and the final half day addressed tasks 5 and 6. The OECD hosted the workshop at its headquarters in Paris. The entire workshop discussions were recorded, but not for attribution, with the exception of the invited presenters on the first day of the meeting. The workshop presentations and discussions were subsequently summarized and edited, and U.S. National Committee for CODATA produced this report in collaboration with the OECD. We hope that the report will contribute to the improvement of methods and techniques for obtaining a better understanding of different policies for managing public sector information online.

Roberta Balstad
Chair, Project Steering Committee
Columbia University

Paul F. Uhlir
Project Co-Director
The National Academies

Graham Vickery
Project Co-Director
Organisation for Economic Co-operation and Development

Acknowledgments

The U.S. National Committee for CODATA and the Board on International Scientific Organizations of the National Research Council of the National Academies wish to express their sincere thanks to the many individuals who played significant roles in planning the international workshop, The Socioeconomic Effects of Public Sector Information on Digital Networks: Toward a Better Understanding of Different Access and Reuse Policies. The workshop steering committee was chaired by Roberta Balstad of Columbia University, and the other members of the committee were Christine Borgman of the University of California at Los Angeles, John Houghton of the University of Melbourne in Australia, Harlan Onsrud of the University of Maine, and Knut Rexed of Rexed & Spröndly AB, Sweden. We also would like to thank the experts who made presentations during the workshop, who are listed in the table of contents below, as well as the session chairs and rapporteurs who are listed in the meeting agenda in Appendix A.

This report has been reviewed in draft form by individuals chosen for their diverse perspectives and technical expertise, in accordance with procedures approved by the National Academies' Report Review Committee. The purpose of this independent review is to provide candid and critical comments that will assist the institution in making its published report as sound as possible and to ensure that the report meets institutional standards for quality and objectivity. The review comments and draft manuscript remain confidential to protect the integrity of the process.

We wish to thank the following individuals for their review of this report: Antti Eskola, Ministry of Employment and the Economy, Finland; Anne Fitzgerald, Queensland University of Technology; Jeff Lazo, National Center for Atmospheric Research; Knut Rexed, Ministry of Finance, Sweden (Retired); and J. Timothy Sprehe, Sprehe Information Management Associates.

Although the reviewers listed above have provided many constructive comments and suggestions, they were not asked to endorse the content of the report, nor did they see the final draft before its release. Responsibility for the final content of this report rests entirely with the author and the institution.

Finally, the U.S. National Committee for CODATA and the OECD would like to recognize the contributions of the following individuals to the completion of this project and the publication: Tilman Merz helped to organize the meeting at the OECD, and Chad Abel-Kops and Daniel Cohen, both on assignment to the National Academies from the U.S. Library of Congress, assisted with the editing and the production of the manuscript.

Contents

PART ONE

                                          Page

1. Introduction   1
   Paul Uhlir, The National Academies
   United States

2. Overview of U.S. Federal Government Information Policy   3
   Nancy Weiss, Institute of Museum and Library Services
   United States

3. PSI Implementation in the UK: Successes and Challenges   7
   Jim Wretham, Office of Public Sector Information
   United Kingdom

4. The Value to Industry of PSI: The Business Sector Perspective   10
   Martin Fornefeld, MICUS Management Consulting
    Germany

      DISCUSSION BY WORKSHOP PARTICIPANTS   14

5. Achieving Fair and Open Access to PSI for Maximum Returns   17
   Michael Nicholson, PSI Alliance
   United Kingdom

      DISCUSSION BY WORKSHOP PARTICIPANTS   19

PART TWO

6. Public Sector Information: Why Bother?   25
   Robbin te Velde, Dialogic
   The Netherlands

7. Measuring the Economic Impact of the PSI Directive in the Context of the 2008 Review   29
   Chris Corbin, ePSIplus
   United Kingdom

8. Different PSI Access Policies and Their Impact   31
   Frederika Welle Donker, Delft University of Technology
   The Netherlands

9. The Price of Everything but the Value of Nothing   37
   Antoinette Graves, Office of Fair Trading
   United Kingdom

10. Enhancing Access to Government Information: Economic Theory as It Applies to Statistics Canada   40
    Kirsti Nilsen, University of Western Ontario
    Canada

11. Assessing the Impact of Public Sector Geographic Information   45
    Max Craglia, Institute for Environment and Sustainability, JRC
    Italy

12. Assessing the Economic and Social Benefits of NOAA Data Online   47
    Rodney Weiher, NOAA
    United States

13. Exploring the Impacts of Enhanced Access to Publicly Funded Research   51
    John Houghton, Victoria University
    Australia

        DISCUSSION BY WORKSHOP PARTICIPANTS   56

PART THREE

14. Measuring the Social and Economic Costs of Public Sector Information Online: A Review of the Literature and Future Directions   61
    Paul F. Uhlir, Raed M. Sharif, and Tilman Merz

15. Summary of the First Breakout Session   69
    Juan Carlos de Martin, Rapporteur

16. Summary of the Second Breakout Session   73
    Tilman Merz, Rapporteur

PART FOUR

17. General Discussion of Results from the Breakout Sessions and Possible Next Steps   75
    Paul F. Uhlir, Rapporteur

APPENDIXES

A.   Workshop Agenda   83

B.   Biographical Summaries of Workshop Chairs, Presenters, and Rapporteurs   87

PART ONE

1. Introduction

Paul Uhlir
The National Academies, United States

Governments generate vast amounts of digital data and information, and increasingly they are disseminating it online. The Organisation for Economic Co-operation and Development (OECD) defines public sector information as having characteristics of being "dynamic and continually generated, directly generated by the public sector, associated with the functioning of the public sector (for example, meteorological data, business statistics), and readily useable in commercial applications…".[1] The OECD distinguishes PSI from "public content", which it characterizes as being "static (i.e., it is an established record), held by the public sector rather than being generated by it (cultural archives, artistic works where third-party rights may be important), not directly associated with the functioning of government, and not necessarily associated with commercial uses but having other public good purposes (culture, education)"[2].

Most governments have initiatives of various kinds for promoting the use of the Internet as a way of disseminating their information products to the public. Governments use legislative and regulatory (administrative) mechanisms to implement policies concerning access to and reuse of this PSI. Some of these policies extend across the entire government, while others are specific to certain types of information or agencies within the government.

Governments throughout the world have different approaches to how they make their PSI available and the terms under which the information may be reused. Access policies vary greatly, from fully open access to access that is restricted in various ways, and provided either without charge or at some cost to the user. Reuse policies range from allowing unrestricted reuse to imposing a broad range of restrictions. Furthermore, the variations on access and reuse policies and conditions vary not only across national governments, but also in many cases within each country at the state and local levels. There also appears to be significant variability in the implementation and enforcement of these access and reuse policies.

At the same time, there appears to be a broad recognition in both the public and private sectors of the importance of digital networks and PSI to the economy and to society. The public investment in PSI in the United States alone has been estimated to be in the tens of billions of dollars. The intangible, non-market social benefits of different types of PSI are harder to measure, but they also can be very significant. They include educational, research, good-governance, and various other benefits that help improve the

---

[1] OECD. 2006. *Digital Broadband Content: Public Sector Information and Content*. Paris: OECD, p. 8.
[2] Ibid.

welfare of society. Many other countries also have large investments in generating and disseminating PSI and an interest in stimulating greater rates of socioeconomic returns from those activities. Some very large PSI programs, such as the Global Earth Observation System of Systems, are not just national programs but are coordinated and utilized on a global basis, and there are many others whose scope and potential effects are smaller but still significant.

Despite the huge investments in PSI and the even larger estimated effects, surprisingly little is known about the costs and benefits of different information policies on the information society and the knowledge economy. There is relatively little empirical data available on the effects of PSI disseminated on the Internet or on the different policy approaches to this dissemination, and what data do exist are generally neither detailed nor comprehensive. Small changes in access and use conditions may have large consequences. By understanding the strengths and weaknesses of the current assessment methods and their underlying criteria, it should be possible to improve and apply such tools to help rationalize the policies and to clarify the special role of the internet in disseminating PSI. This in turn can help promote the efficiency and effectiveness of PSI investments and management, and to improve their downstream economic and social results. Therefore, there is an urgent need to identify, understand, and evaluate the current methods and underlying criteria that are used in this area in order to provide a more solid framework for making such policies.

The workshop that is summarized in this report was intended to review the state of the art in assessment methods and to improve the understanding of what is known and what needs to be known about the effects of PSI activities. Part One provides some background on the goals, values, and the policy perspectives of government PSI producers, one in Europe and one in the United States, as well as of the users of PSI in industry. Part Two offers a number of examples of assessment methods used by those who study the effects of placing PSI online.

Part Three summarizes a discussion of what the different elements of the methodologies are and what might be done to improve them. We begin with a brief overview of the literature and of some of the strengths and weaknesses associated with the current methodologies. This presentation also provides some suggestions for discussion of future work in this area. Following the overview, there were two moderated breakout discussions at the workshop, one focused on the producers from the public sector and one on the users' perspectives. We designated rapporteurs who synthesized those discussions and which are summarized in this report. In Part Four, the rapporteur provides a summary of the subsequent plenary discussion and identifies some next steps.

2. Overview of U.S. Federal Government Information Policy[1]

Nancy Weiss
Institute of Museum and Library Services, United States

Information policy in the United States has a long history, dating back to the establishment of the nation. The founding fathers, who drafted the U.S. Constitution and the country's early laws, faced significant information policy and access challenges. They had helped to establish a new democracy—with a government of the people, for the people, and by the people—in a country in which people were widely dispersed and generally uneducated. They needed to create different mechanisms of communication and information dissemination in order to promote trade and economic development. They also had to ensure that individuals were able to obtain the information and skills necessary to participate meaningfully in their own governance. As James Madison, one of the founders, said, "A popular government without popular information or the means of acquiring it is but a prologue to a farce, or a tragedy, or both."

As a result, in the United States we have a long cultural and social history of supporting and encouraging public access to information, an attitude that is closely linked with our constitutional and statutory guarantees of freedom of expression, freedom of the press, transparent governance, and democracy. From the beginning, our nation recognized that access to and use of information benefits the nation's citizens as well as the broader global community by promoting the advancement of knowledge, cultural understanding, economic growth, and the general welfare of society.

Of course, access to government information is just as important to nations with highly developed technological and industrial capacity as it was to the United States in the late 1700s. Governments today create vast amounts of information with economic and social value, including but not limited to consumer information, statistical compilations, and information for academic and scientific uses. This presentation provides a brief overview of the public sector information policies and practices in the United States.

There are numerous federal laws that govern access to U.S. government information, ranging from a right to information provided under the Freedom of Information Act and the right to know what is going on in the government, guaranteed by the Sunshine in Government Act, to the United States Copyright Act and a host of others. U.S. federal government information policy is synthesized in a document called Office of Management and Budget Circular A-130, which sets forth a number of general principles that government agencies are supposed to apply when dealing with government information:

- Government information is a valuable national resource. It provides the public with knowledge of the government, society, and economy—past, present, and future. It is a means to ensure the accountability of government, to manage the

---

[1] Based on a presentation found at http://www.oecd.org/dataoecd/28/0/40047022.pdf

government's operations, to maintain the healthy performance of the economy, and is itself a commodity in the marketplace.

- The free flow of information between the government and the public is essential to a democratic society. It is also essential that the government minimize the Federal paperwork burden on the public, minimize the cost of its information activities, and maximize the usefulness of government information.

- In order to minimize the cost and maximize the usefulness of government information, the expected public and private benefits derived from government information should exceed the public and private costs of the information, recognizing that the benefits to be derived from government information may not always be quantifiable.

- The nation can benefit from government information disseminated both by Federal agencies and by diverse nonfederal parties, including State and local government agencies, educational and other not-for-profit institutions, and for-profit organizations.

- Because the public disclosure of government information is essential to the operation of a democracy, the management of Federal information resources should protect the public's right of access to government information.

- The open and efficient exchange of scientific and technical government information, subject to applicable national security controls and the proprietary rights of others, fosters excellence in scientific research and effective use of Federal research and development funds.

In addition to these principles setting forth the importance of public exchange and access to government information, Circular A-130 also contains policies that describe how to avoid restrictive practices. A government agency should avoid establishing or permitting others to have arrangements that are exclusive, restricted, or otherwise interfere with making information available on a timely and equitable basis. That does not imply, however, that a person or entity may not take government information, repackage it, and make it available commercially. Indeed, that is the desired outcome—that a variety of products be developed from the underlying government information. But, generally speaking, government information cannot be transferred to one corporation or private entity without also making it available to others.

Government agencies also operate with the understanding that public access to government information is important and that they should avoid unnecessary restrictions or regulations limiting such access. For example, an agency must avoid charging a fee or royalties on the reuse, resale, or dissemination of government information. Indeed, Circular A-130 encourages agencies to set user fees for government information products at the marginal cost of dissemination. (The Circular provides that the calculation of user charges must exclude the costs associated with the original collection and processing of the information.) As a result, agencies often post information on the Internet, where the marginal cost of dissemination is zero.

The U.S. Copyright Act affects another area of public information policy. Under Section 105 of the copyright law, works created by federal government employees within the scope of their employment are part of the public domain. This policy has contributed to the development of a very robust public domain and to the unfettered reuse of information. In fact, the federal government is the largest producer of public domain information in the United States. Another important factor is that in the United States it is not possible to copyright facts or ideas, whether produced by government or in the private sector. This, too, encourages the broad dissemination and reuse of information.

The United States recognizes many legal, economic, and other public policy reasons for placing government-generated information in the public domain, subject to conditions of open availability and unrestricted reuse. First, a government entity requires no incentive from exclusive property rights to create information, unlike authors or publishers in the private sector. Second, government-generated information is a public good. The public has already paid for the collection of the information through its taxes, and so it should not have to pay a second time when accessing the information. Third, the democratic values and transparency of government would be undermined by restricting citizens from access to and use of public sector information. Finally, information is not an exhaustible resource. Multiple people can use the same data or information for different purposes, without diminishing the value of the information.

Of course, there are some countervailing policies in practice that limit the access to government information. These are generally based on national security concerns and the need to protect personal privacy and confidential information. The government generally protects the proprietary rights of information that has originated from the private sector and been made available for government use.

One recent noteworthy development in the area of access to government-funded (as compared to government-produced) information is legislation that was just passed, after several years of development, that applies to research supported by the U.S. National Institutes of Health (NIH). In 2003 the NIH instituted a data-sharing policy that required any recipient of grant funds totaling more than $500,000 in any single year to include with its grant application a data-sharing plan describing how the research data would be disseminated to the public. Subsequently the NIH adopted a policy that requested, but did not require, investigators to submit an electronic version of the final manuscript of whatever study resulted from the publicly funded research to a central repository of the NIH called PubMed Central.

In order to further encourage the practice of making this information openly available to the public, the U.S. Congress passed a law in late 2007 that requires researchers to deposit a copy of any journal articles resulting from NIH-funded research to this central database within 12 months of the official date of publication. The goal of the law is to derive the greatest possible socioeconomic benefits from information that has been generated with federal government investment by promoting access to that information to any citizens who can use this research information and to other researchers who are trying to advance particular areas of science or to accelerate innovation.

There are many different federal agencies within the United States that provide access to their information. Their policies for information access tend to be mission driven, that is, related to whatever the agency is trying to accomplish. Although there are a number of different areas of emphasis, most federal agencies stress creating an environment that is open and that minimizes barriers to access. As we look at the social and economic impacts of public sector information online, it is important to understand the motivations and the drivers of each agency.

To summarize, U.S. policy has a default rule of open availability and reuse of public sector information with the goal of maximizing the benefits of the public investment made in producing that information. Government information is normally placed in the public domain, reflecting a belief in the public's right to access and reuse government information. U.S. policy promotes the dissemination of government information at no more than marginal costs as well as balancing the many different interests in adopting any new laws without limiting the public's access to public sector information. As Thomas Jefferson, one of the country's founding fathers, explained, "Information is the currency of democracy." U.S. policy continues to build on this core principle.

3. PSI Implementation in the United Kingdom: Successes and Challenges[1]

Jim Wretham
Office of Public Sector Information, United Kingdom

This presentation provides a brief overview of what has been happening recently in the United Kingdom with regard to public sector information (PSI), including what lessons have been learned and, perhaps more important, what the principal challenges are. Over the past ten years or so, there has been an increasing interest in PSI. Before that time, the reuse of such information was of interest to only a select few—to those in the information industry, to publishers, and to those who were interested in the subject because of copyright and licensing issues. But in the United Kingdom and, more generally, throughout the Western world, this is now all changing. Public sector information appears to be grabbing the public's imagination. Why is this?

First of all, in the United Kingdom, as in many other countries, there is a very well established and thriving information industry. Many of the organizations or companies in this industry rely heavily on public sector information.

Second, the Internet is affording to society a great variety of new opportunities. The ability to access and manipulate data is increasingly greater than it has been in the past, and that trend looks as if it will continue.

And third, in the United Kingdom, as well as in other parts of Western Europe in particular, there has been a growing emphasis on legislation concerning access to PSI, or freedom of information laws. So the public is now increasingly thinking of access to information as being a democratic right. This is a tremendously important development.

There have been many milestones in the evolution of the reuse of public sector information. One of the major ones in Europe was the issuance of the European Union Directive on Reuse of Public Sector Information. The United Kingdom put this directive into effect in 2005, and it supported the law by producing a guide to best practices. This guide is still a work in progress.

The United Kingdom has seen a number of successes in this area, and these successes have depended on different factors. One of these factors, at least as far as central government information is concerned, is the fact that most government information is licensed by the Office of Public Sector Information (OPSI). This makes it possible to have a "one stop shop."

The OPSI has developed the *click use license*, which is an online licensing system that was set up about seven years ago and has produced some good results. There are now about 14,000 of these licenses worldwide. People can access and reuse a great amount

---

[1] Based on a presentation found at http://www.oecd.org/dataoecd/28/3/40046991.pdf

and variety of information generated by the public sector. Nevertheless, there is some room for liberalizing this further, for example, by moving away from the current demand that a person must register before being allowed to access and reuse information.

The OPSI also has developed a system known as the information fair trader scheme (IFTS). The system is intended to produce and promulgate standards across the public sector, to acknowledge best practices for encouraging fairness, transparency, and openness, and to make sure that organizations have the proper processes in place. The OPSI operates two versions of the information fair trader scheme. The more comprehensive version is aimed at major traders of public sector information, such as organizations that produce mapping or meteorological data. They use the full IFTS accreditation, which involves the OPSI sending experts into these organizations to review practices and processes. Not all holders of PSI are major traders, however, so the OPSI has identified and developed an online assessment process that is much simpler and that is aimed at these smaller users.

Working with representatives from industry and other parts of the public sector, the OPSI has also created an advisory panel on public sector information. This advisory panel provides an independent focus for the producers of PSI, who represent the interests of the information industry. These producers of PSI also are instrumental in identifying trends, providing research, and informing those in OPSI about the best approaches to the reuse of public sector information. This advisory panel is carrying out a very important function.

The OPSI also is looking at ways in which to improve access to PSI. Working with the information industry, the organization has initiated a number of different activities aimed at helping people access information more easily and at teaching them how to use the Web and the various automatic tools available for searching for and connecting with information. Of course, this is a long journey, and major challenges lie ahead.

One of the most important challenges is to make sure that there is a correct balance between the various trading models and some of the public sector organizations. In the United Kingdom is a set of organizations known as trading funds. Although a trading fund is an operation of a government department, these organizations enjoy a certain amount of self sufficiency in terms of funding, and they are encouraged to behave in a commercial manner. There are some challenges to setting up this model, and it is important to make sure that the balance is right.

A second challenge, which is identified in the EU PSI Directive, concerns the definition of a public task. This definition needs further refinement so that its meaning is precisely clear. A public task refers to activities that are regarded as being part of the public sector organization's mission. The consequences of activities falling within the organization's public task are limits on the extent to which that organization may operate in the information reuse domain itself as a producer of value-added products or services.

A third challenge concerns the "no obligation" aspect of the PSI directive, which is reflected in U.K. regulations as well. In the public sector, as perhaps in all of life, unless people have to do something, they tend not to do it. So the fact that there is no obligation to allow reuse has tended to lead many public sector organizations to bury their heads in the sand and to say that reuse is not for them to worry about. There is no quick and easy solution to this other than to make sure that the OPSI encourages and publicizes the benefits of reuse of public sector information.

Getting this message across will require the use of many resources, notably from the OPSI, which is only a small part of the government. There are about 100,000 public sector organizations in the United Kingdom, so getting that message across will not be easy. Resources will be important.

A final challenge centers on awareness and impact—raising awareness through training and then measuring the impact, that is, what the economic benefits of PSI use are. The PSI Discussion Forum is a private-public initiative in this area. It has opened up the debate across the public and private sectors and recently received some favorable coverage in the press. The OPSI also developed a Web channel to deal with requests by people wanting to reuse public sector information.

Maintaining standards is, of course, highly important as well. The OPSI works closely with some of the audit bodies so that it has experts available who can go into public sector organizations and test what is actually happening in the reuse field. The OPSI works closely with the United Kingdom's Office of Fair Trading (OFT) in the areas of competition and how markets operate. The OPSI plans to do some spot audits on public sector information. There is a major focus on government reviews, and some independent economic analysis has been commissioned that will look at how the various models across the United Kingdom operate. That analysis is expected to provide some guidance for the future.

Two key reports have been released over the past eighteen months. One was on the commercial use of public information and was produced by the OFT.[2] The second was the *Power of Information*[3] review. Although both of these reports deal with the reuse of public information, they come at it from somewhat different perspectives. The OFT report takes the point of view of a commercial reuser, looking at how to add value to this huge resource in order to benefit the economy. The *Power of Information* review, on the other hand, focuses mainly on the benefits of PSI to the citizen. It looks at how the Internet gives everyone the opportunity to use information in ways that were not possible just 10 years ago, using applications such as data mashing, or integrating, and it examines ways in which citizens can take information and share it with like-minded individuals. One example in the *Power of Information* described people who had visited restaurants in Los Angeles and who then shared information about the standards of the food, cleanliness, and other factors. One result of this activity was to elevate the standards across those restaurants.

In conclusion, the U.K. government is working to achieve three objectives. First, it seeks to embrace the information needs of the citizen. Second, it is attempting to encourage information reuse and commercial exploitation. And finally, it wishes to create easy-to-find and easy-to-use public sector information.

---

[2] http://www.opsi.gov.uk/advice/poi/oft-cupi.pdf
[3] http://www.opsi.gov.uk/advice/poi/power-of-information-review.pdf

4. The Value to Industry of PSI: The Business Sector Perspective[1]

Martin Fornefeld
MICUS Management Consulting, Germany

This presentation discusses the value of PSI to industry from the perspective of the business sector. MICUS is a management consulting company based in Düsseldorf and Berlin. Besides management consulting, it focuses on e-government projects for the German federal government and market studies. In particular, MICUS does many market studies concerning PSI and the economic value of innovation. Its clients generally come from the public sector, the energy sector, and the service sector. MICUS plans to publish three studies in 2008: Business Models for German Companies in International Geo-Information Markets; The Impact of Broadband and Growth in Productivity; and The Assessment of the Reuse of Public Sector Information in the Geographical Information, Meteorological Information, and Legal Information Sectors.

What are the problems in obtaining PSI in Germany today? Negotiations about PSI reuse often fail. The private sector is requesting new pricing and licensing models for PSI reuse throughout Europe, but these requests for easier and more liberal licensing models and lower prices for the procurement of PSI have not been very successful. There are barriers to PSI reuse. There is insufficient market transparency by the PSI holders who are responsible for the data. And despite strong demand there have been a number of bad experiences, such as those that happened in securing data for maps, which have resulted in the gradual emergence of economical alternatives from private sources.

There are also barriers on the PSI holders' side, especially the lack of knowledge about how the market works and a tendency to overestimate the value of their products. In the meteorological market, for example, there are now parallel infrastructures in Germany, with weather stations maintained by the National Meteorological Service and similar stations maintained by private industry. This happened only after negotiations with the German government for PSI reuse failed. Because data production is costly, the government believes that the corresponding price must also be set high, and so the distribution network does not work. Consequently, there remain many unexploited business opportunities.

In Germany the market for geo-information increased from €1 billion in 2000 to €1.6 billion in 2006. What is especially interesting is how this is divided. In 2000 the emphasis was on planning and maintenance systems, from which utility and engineering companies bought a great deal of cadastral[2] information. However, by 2004 the navigation market had exploded, and two years later more than 50 percent of the demand for geo-information was being driven by the navigation market, much of this based on "free" private data (cf., Intergraph, Google Earth).

---

[1] Based on a presentation found at http://www.oecd.org/dataoecd/27/9/40047551.pdf

[2] Merriam-Webster defines cadastre as "an official register of the quantity, value, and ownership of real estate used in apportioning taxes." 2009. In *Merriam-Webster Online Dictionary*. Retrieved February 12, 2009, from http://www.merriam-webster.com/dictionary/cadastre.

At about the same time, in 2007, the German government's revenue from PSI was only €164,000. That revenue came from three main areas: legal information, vehicle information, and meteorological data. Meanwhile, cartography, statistics, medical information, geo-information, and environmental information from the government garnered little revenue. Although the market indicates that statistics and cartographic information have more potential value, the government did not appear to take advantage of this potential.

So what is the value of PSI? In discussing this, it is important to remember that the source data are only the starting point. For each application that puts these data to work and for every additional function and data set one adds, the value is increased—a higher step on the value chain. For a complex combination of data like statistics and geographical data, the value of the source data is increased by, say, a factor of five. And with information-based services like mapping, geocoding, and analyzing tools or applications, that factor may be 10. The further along the value chain, the greater the value that can be assigned to the data. This process of adding value is done by the private market. The PSI holder should make the offer, and the rest should be done by the service provider.

This is called value chain production. The value of the source data are quite low, but the costs of the source data in most cases are quite high. So how do we discover the value of the additional factors? In 2007 we had the chance to observe bids on some companies that provided cartographic data, such as Tele Atlas and Navteq. TomTom was bidding on Tele Atlas, and Nokia was bidding on Navteq, and the prices being discussed were about €2-3 billion for Tele Atlas and nearly €6 billion for Navteq. That was about ten times the annual sales of these companies.

Tele Atlas was not even profitable. TomTom's profit in 2006 was €22 million, on sales of €1.8 billion. The interesting thing was that although the Tele Atlas and Navteq data maps were their own maps, the companies had bought the original maps from public bodies in the late 1990s. Afterwards, they added their own updates and digitized the data, and today these maps are proprietary and well along the value chain. There have been two other interesting acquisitions in the industry. Pitney Bowes bought MapInfo, a geomarketing software company, and Microsoft just bought Multimap, a Web map provider, for two to five times the annual sales.

Meanwhile, the reuse of geographical PSI lags, so what would be the right strategy for the PSI holder to open the PSI market? To answer that question we developed a performance matrix that facilitates strategic development. On one side we list PSI availability and quality of services (including usability of web services) from low to high. On the other side we list the price for PSI from low to high.

FIGURE 1: Slide 11 from presentation of Martin Fornefeld, MICUS Management Consulting, Germany.

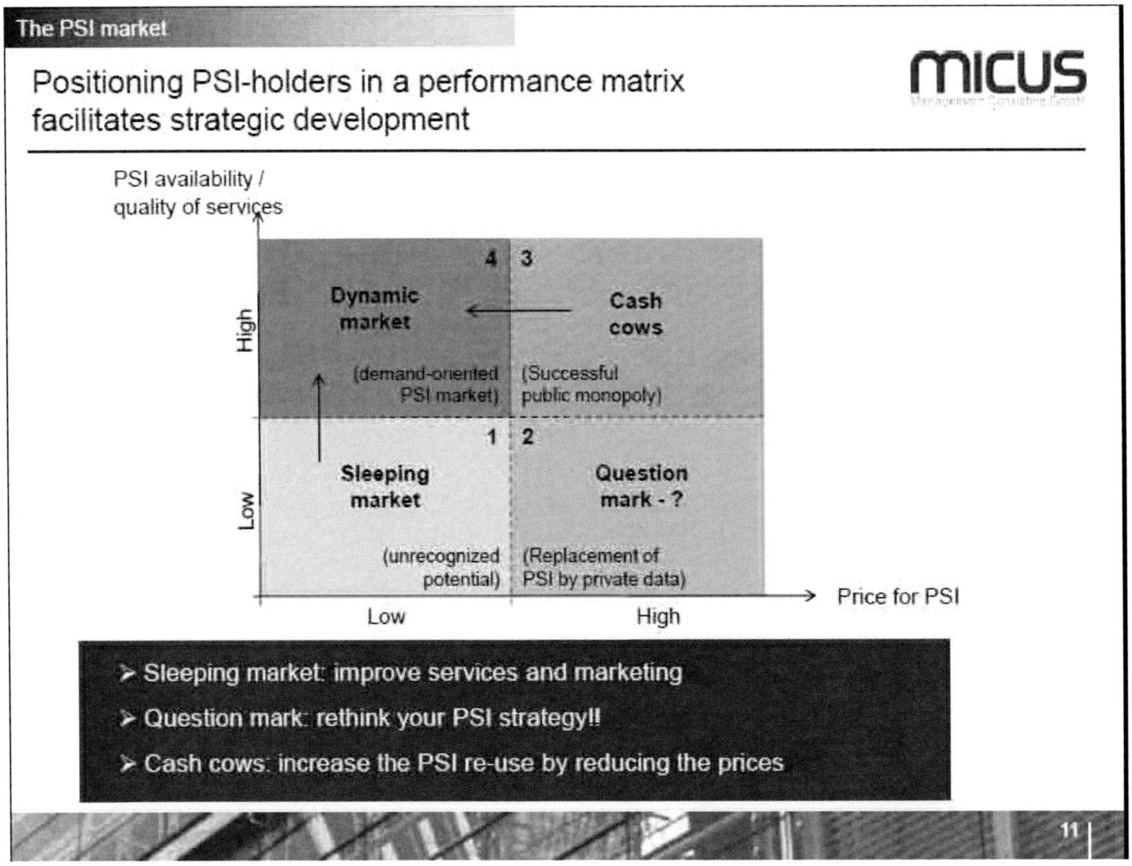

Source: http://www.oecd.org/dataoecd/27/9/40047551.pdf

Within the graph are four squares, the first being a sleeping market, that is, one with unrecognized potential. This unrecognized potential includes statistical information that has not yet been marketed. The second square holds a question mark representing a situation characterized by the question, Why do we see high prices but low availability and low quality of services? This is a market where replacement of PSI by private data may take place. The third square is a cash cow, e.g., a situation with high prices, high availability, and good service. This represents a successful public monopoly; an example would be Juris GmbH, a data-sharing plan in Germany that holds a monopoly on legal information, with high prices and high availability. The fourth square is the ideal of what we would wish to achieve in a dynamic market—high availability, low prices, and a demand-oriented PSI market. EuroLex, another European provider of legal information, is a good example.

So what strategies can we offer for these four squares? First, a sleeping market needs improvement in services and marketing. One needs to rethink the PSI strategy here. That is, is there a need anymore for a public service, or can it be replaced with a private service? The cash cows in the third square can increase the reuse of PSI by reducing prices and finding new customers, but are low prices for PSI a risk for the public service?

In my opinion, no; rather, the risk is if you do not change your pricing policy at all. If we continue with the pricing models now in use across Europe, the sales will go down. Private alternatives may be found to substitute for PSI products.

Moreover, if one reduces prices, this will increase PSI and sales, and, in the short term, the price reduction will be compensated by the increasing demand. For example, Austria reduced prices last year, and many new customers have been found there. Thus, reducing prices and enhancing the availability of PSI will lead to a dynamic market.

In summary, what is our advice for better PSI reuse? First, one should raise awareness of the potential for PSI in the reuse of private sector information. There is a huge unexploited potential with a high economic impact. Exploiting the potential in the PSI market requires lower pricing and less restrictive licensing agreements. To be sure, there is no such thing as a free lunch. Reusable, high-quality information requires investment. There is also a need for innovative business models that consider the whole value chain. These models must be aware of product substitution. Finally, there is a need to rethink and review public services. If product substitution occurs, the question becomes: Is there still a demand for the public service, or may it be replaced by a private service?

DISCUSSION BY WORKSHOP PARTICIPANTS

PARTICIPANT: Typically the costs of buying or acquiring PSI are really a small part of the costs for the reuser, perhaps 1, 2, or 3 percent. So why bother about decreasing the price if it is just such a small part of the costs anyway? Is it not more in the quality of the data where the pain is? Dr. Fornefeld stated that if one reduces the price, the demand goes up and everyone will be happy. But if only 1 percent of the reuser's costs are in PSI, the effects will not be that strong, unless price elasticity is very strong.

DR. FORNEFELD: We have to use intelligent, innovative business models to increase the reuse of data. It is not a question of whether there should be a price, but there should be a market price, and that is a problem especially for the public body. What is the market price? A public body cannot calculate the market price, but public-private partnerships can help to define it.

PARTICIPANT: From the perspective of the European Commission, the important thing is to maximize the value of PSI. The earnings for the public bodies that charge only the marginal costs are very limited. Those bodies that have succeeded are those that have high licensing prices and high earnings. But this is only one way of seeing things. Perhaps one can have much more success if there are much lower earnings but a high degree of use because a very active reuse market has been created.

The Commission has a license, a reuse policy, in which we do not charge at all for such uses as EuroLex. Very recently we put our language resources online—gigabytes of pairs of languages from machine translations that allow translations into 23 languages. These resources, which are unique, are works of a team of, I would say, thousands of translators during many, many years. This is something for which it is very difficult to substitute the work of private companies.

We put it on the Web. We issued a press release, and we had between 1,000 and 1,500 downloads of the whole dataset in the first week. So I would offer the message of thinking in these terms about the value derived from making the work of public sector organizations freely available. For a public sector body, or at least for the Commission, talking about a business model seems inappropriate, because we are not a commercial business. You may talk about financing models, and then we would have to talk with the financial ministers, but to talk about business models seems to me a very one-sided way to see things, and perhaps this is part of the problem. Thinking in terms of business models when the context is not a real business creates some of the challenges.

For my last comment, I would encourage everybody to come forward with examples of what Dr. Fornefeld mentioned; that is, whether usage increases if you diminish your licensing costs or the cost of PSI. If this can be proven to be the case with examples, that would be, as you say in Britain, the proof of the pudding being in the eating.

So we have established that you really can provide geographical information this way. If there were sufficient examples perhaps there would be no further need to be here discussing it, as the proposition would be so straightforward. That would leave simply the question of implementation. Of course, this brings us to another issue that we will be talking about, which was mentioned previously in the United States, and that is the question of quality.

In the United States, of course, there are also critics of the lack of funding from the national agencies in some areas, especially in geographical information. The critics argue that the government data is of limited value, so if you really want good data you have to go to the private sector to buy it. In the end, perhaps PSI is free or available at only marginal cost, but the value of it is limited for certain applications. That is another debate, however.

PARTICIPANT: Dr. Fornefeld mentioned the importance of private-public partnerships and the possibility of determining a price. One of the experiences we have had with geographical information in the European Union, for instance, is that there have been a number of public-private partnerships working since the mid-1990s, and they have been fairly successful in terms of their data quality and the distribution of data among the major players. When one has established successful models like that, however, changing them later on to allow access for everybody and dismantle the barriers inevitably put up by the public-private partnership can lead to a problem.

So, there is no such thing as a free lunch in this trade off. It would be interesting for us to hear if all the governments have been in that position and what they have done.

PARTICIPANT: I found the question raised by the European Commission quite interesting and a crucial one. Are we talking about a business model or a business case? Are we as governments or public authorities talking about cost recovery when actually the business side is clearly thinking in terms of a business model and making something profitable? I think as policymakers we have certain policy imperatives. This discussion does remind me of some of the work we did on e-government both at the national and the European levels, but also work at the OECD when we were looking at the business case for e-government and we had a clear policy imperative. We were pushing information and communication technologies into the public sector and thereby indirectly encouraging the adoption of the new technologies—the new media and the Internet.

This is very much along the same lines, but we are going maybe one step further, which is that we are contributing to innovation, to growth, and to productivity. Research by the OECD has proved that already, but I think it will be interesting to see how we can transform—or whether we need to transform—the way of thinking in the public sector, where thinking about a business model is still foreign. It would be helpful to have a good quantification of how we do that both in terms of recovering costs from the public sector and also knowing how much effort we should put into it because we know what the end game may be.

But that was supposed to be only a side comment, and I actually had a question for Dr. Fornefeld, which was that I was very interested in the map that he showed about the weather system in Germany. I was just wondering if he could elaborate on why the talks between the public authority and the private entity broke down. I wonder whether there are some lessons that we can take from this particular case study as to how we could improve collaboration between the public and private sectors in PSI.

DR. FORNEFELD: How did it work with the weather stations in Germany? There have always been, and still are, a lot of discussions about pricing of the meteorological data from the DWD, the German meteorological government agency. The private meteorological providers complain that there is a natural monopoly, especially on the data from satellites, that affects the prices. What is the right price for satellite photos for the weather station information? Due to the inability of the DWD to resolve this pricing question, the whole effort to provide this PSI meteorological data did not succeed. When the DWD could not determine the price at which to make the data available to the private meteorological data providers, the private data providers built their own grid of weather stations. This experience led to some critical discussions about public monopolies and the power of a natural monopoly in setting prices.

5. Achieving Fair and Open Access to PSI for Maximum Returns[1]

Michael Nicholson
PSI Alliance, United Kingdom

The PSI Alliance is an association of private sector PSI reusers, located primarily in Europe. My own knowledge is of the situation in the United Kingdom.

Public sector information is an enormously underexploited market throughout Europe. In general, innovative PSI reuse is being driven by small companies. In the United Kingdom it is relatively easy to communicate with PSI holders, but in other countries this is not always the case. In all countries the reactions from PSI holders to proposals for reuse vary from holder to holder.

For example, the Environment Agency in the United Kingdom has stated that while it *could* create a list of the agency's PSI and make it available to potential users, such a move would cost money which may be better used in flood defenses. "Would you prefer data or flooding?" is the question they asked. Other PSI discussions have run into the issue of public safety and security. For instance, the Coal Authority holds information on underground workings—undoubtedly PSI—which could be made available to the public. If this were done, however, hundreds of thousands of homeowners might be appalled to discover that there are mines some 500 feet below their houses. They would assume the worst, despite being entirely secure in most cases.

Many PSI holders are simply unaware of the reuse opportunity. Some PSI holders do little to encourage reuse; others positively obstruct it. They either consider PSI to be "their" data, the "citizens' data," or anyone else's data except the private sector's ("All they will do is profit from it"). Some PSI holders see making the data available as a low priority; others see it as vitally important; and still others want to exploit the PSI themselves. In the United Kingdom, for example, the focus in the areas of geospatial and meteorological data is on revenue protection rather than value maximization. This creates substantial barriers to reuse. Essentially, instead of the tap being turned full on, it is half off. There are also some well-placed and powerful civil servants in charge of organizations that are considered to be national treasures who see no reason to change the status quo. This is an issue that all too often can be dealt with only by the politicians, but it is not a vote-winner and so does not attract their attention. Parts of the U.K. and French establishments are beginning to consider these issues in greater depth, and it will be interesting to see the outcome.

Despite the laggards, some PSI holders are exemplars and actively seek partners for PSI reuse. Entrepreneurs are thus sometimes welcomed and sometimes resisted. Remember, however, that if there is only one obstacle left, this will still prevent PSI from being reused. So in order to increase the value of PSI, all material barriers must be removed. I would suggest that whatever reuse policies are adopted, they must be straightforward. Complex policies will not work.

---

[1] Based on a presentation found at http://www.oecd.org/dataoecd/12/52/40064545.pdf

Small companies report problems with unfair competition arising from poorly defined reuse policies. Some PSI holders that exploit their own data create so many restrictions to protect their own activities that the private sector ends up attempting to develop its own data as an alternative. Apart from the duplicated investment, the risk in this situation is that the PSI holder will then loosen its restrictions, undercutting the private sector's investment and making it potentially worthless.

While Dr. Fornefeld claimed that high prices for PSI were a result of overestimating the value of data, that is not necessarily correct. In my experience, prices can be high simply because those who set them are risk averse and have no competition in a market with no pricing comparisons. There is a reluctance to experiment with the market and to drop prices when there is no competition.

There needs to be a mechanism for countries to define what information must be collected as PSI. It is clearly not acceptable for the public bodies creating PSI to themselves determine what data to collect. Rather, the state has to decide what it needs to own and collect as part of the national information infrastructure and then to decide on its policy for wider distribution. Whatever the state decides to own itself should be very easily accessible. The question should also be asked whether the private sector should be collecting any of this data instead.

The prime minister speaks enthusiastically about how the use of technology has grown in the United Kingdom. It is certainly true that, over the last ten years, software, hardware, bandwidth, and other technologies have improved immeasurably. It is also remarkable what has been achieved with the digitization of public resources. Ten years ago, user skill levels were a real constraint, but today the majority of people can use a computer and the Internet. So the constraints of user skills and technical delivery are no longer the key issues. As these problems have been solved, the most important constraint has instead become access to information. Whatever the costs of limiting access to PSI at present, they can only grow.

These costs of limiting access to PSI fall into three categories. First, there are direct and indirect costs to the public sector, which are generally not measured. If efficiency improved in the public sector by only 1 percent as a result of free or improved access to the geospatial element of PSI (e.g., in the United Kingdom, the Ordnance Survey or the Met Office), the sum saved would be the equivalent of eight times the cost to the state of collecting the data in the first place.

Second, there are costs to the private sector, both direct—excessive time spent negotiating, managing, and complying with licenses or additional costs collecting data that should be openly available—and indirect, such as the loss of opportunity.

Finally, the economic cost to the citizen when knowledge is available, but inaccessible, cannot be overlooked. For instance, in the United Kingdom and France public bodies have created excellent maps, but their license terms do not always allow the ready use of these maps, such as making them available on the Internet. Job opportunities are lost, higher taxes may result, and there is less choice. If U.K. citizens were offered a choice between a continuation of the current situation (cost and restrictive licensing) and one where their taxes would be increased by £1.25 but they had free access to Ordnance Survey maps on the Internet, would they not reach in their pockets for the £1.25?

DISCUSSION BY WORKSHOP PARTICIPANTS

PARTICIPANT: I would like to focus a bit more on the importance of digital networks and the characteristics of digital information in this context. One thing that this discussion so far has not alluded to, much less talked about in any serious way, is the power of networks and network effects that arises from putting information freely online to perhaps a billion Internet users. If you have free information online that is accessible to each person with access to the Internet, one has the potential of a billion entrepreneurs who can take that information and recombine it with other information to create new knowledge and new products and services that are not possible if there are barriers to that knowledge in the form of either a high price of access or reuse restrictions.

One of the fundamental aspects of digital information is that it can be reconfigured and combined with other information to make new information in ways that cannot be anticipated. So the potential always exists of serendipitous results that whoever may be providing the information online cannot fully anticipate. Therefore, in terms of the costs associated with these business models, there may be a tremendous amount of lost opportunity costs that are very difficult to measure and largely hidden but that are related to the fact that there is a great amount of potential social and economic value from the reuse of that information in many unanticipated ways.

I would also like to note that we are flooded with a deluge of information, and a resulting characteristic of digital information on networks is that if one is to make optimum use of it, one needs to do that by automated means. This is because people cannot possibly find, sift through, and process the information themselves. The future of value creation online, therefore, is to handle that information automatically with various kinds of new software tools that are able to extract and recombine the data and information, creating new knowledge and new value from existing information automatically rather than through human intervention.

Both the costs and, in particular, the legal restrictions on reuse are a complete barrier to machine-automated value creation from existing information online. This could certainly be a problem for the policy community with regard to the economic exploitation of information online.

PARTICIPANT: I think the 2007 *Power of Information* report in the United Kingdom really has some very good examples of the big potential of networks, of new uses, and of matching up information.

PARTICIPANT: I would like to get back to something that Michael Nicholson raised very eloquently about the funding problem, since funding is one of the keys. You pointed out that we should develop some clear ideas about what the role of government is in general and then within defined areas, such as mapping, weather information, and the like, to be clear that these are a part of public tasks. Then it is necessary to organize the funding in such a way that those particular roles of government are accomplished well. I would like to get more opinions about that, however, because it was an issue when we were writing the policy principles for public sector information. In fact, there initially was a paragraph about this, but some of the drafters felt it was straying into areas of telling governments what they should do. So it was very hard to write this in a way that one did not get into a philosophical debate about what governments should or should not be doing.

It is a pity in some ways—and I think this is an essential point—which is why we had it in some of the earlier drafts. This debate is not just about access and use, but it is essential to think about what happens if data are given away or sold at very low, marginal cost. What are the incentives then, and how can one structure a system that produces good quality data and then distributes them in a timely fashion if suddenly part of the revenue stream that supported this function is cut off?

I would like to get the participants' opinions about this. Is it really about going back to Parliament to debate this and getting them to fund the PSI activities out of a general purpose tax? Michael Nicholson said it would cost £1.25 per head in the United Kingdom to open up the data held by the Ordnance Survey. An interesting parallel is that in France President Sarkozy launched a debate in January 2008 about how to fund public sector TV. He said that he thought it should not be funded by advertising—which means that now the public sector TV and radio probably have to find about €1.2 billion a year in new revenues, which they did not have to find before because they were supporting part of their activities with advertising. Maybe advertising is something to consider because the BBC is going down the track of thinking more about advertising revenue as well as having a license fee. Is the solution for maintaining the production and dissemination of PSI licensing fees, advertising, or general tax revenues?

PARTICIPANT: In Finland there is a historical burden in the funding model for public sector organizations. It used to be that if you were a public sector organization, a good way to get a project growing steadily and get more staff was if you could invent more public tasks for yourself. But then, in the 1980s or 1990s, there was a trend toward the philosophy that these public sector organizations should earn their living by selling their services, including public sector information, and quite a lot of liberty was given to these public sector organizations to define their own public sector pricing policies.

So in Finland we now have a terrible mess of pricing policies, different public sector organizations charging different kinds of fees and with different policies. Now that the EU PSI directive has come into force and there is some political pressure for changing the system, our Finance Ministry is, or seems to be, quite reluctant to touch this mess because their first question has been: What would be the increase in revenue or public good that we would gain from unifying these pricing policies? If you cannot calculate it or if you say that it is, for instance, €50 million a year, we will not touch it because this is a too small an issue for an organization as important as the Finance Ministry. So this is a problem: How to convince the Finance Ministry to interfere with the independence of our public sector organizations and to also risk upsetting the precarious situation that has been created by giving all these public sector organizations such broad discretion to define their own pricing policies. I do not have a solution, but rather, I am raising the issue.

PARTICIPANT: I do not have a solution, either. I think it is absolutely right that in the United Kingdom there has been a huge amount of thought given to this, but part of the problem is that the thinking has not been translated into action. What I would say is that my rather rudimentary examination of the accounts of some of these trading funds in the United Kingdom suggests that the actual costs of licensing, pricing, and managing the PSI is far higher than one would normally expect. I was very interested to see that when there were some changes made in this regard in Australia, the actual cost of distribution went down when the process became simplified.

PARTICIPANT: Actually, there is very little hard statistical evidence to back up this assertion.

PARTICIPANT: Well, there is absolute evidence that in the United Kingdom the cost of the organizations would go down if licensing were not a factor. I think there is a much bigger issue though about what they should be doing in the first place. It is a very awkward question. But in a sense I think we have to find a way in the United Kingdom of making sure that there is a way of getting to the answer without asking the people who are providing the data. It has to be something where instead of asking the last executioner if abolishing capital punishment is a good idea or not, you actually find some better way of establishing what governments should be collecting for their own needs.

PARTICIPANT: May I just follow up on the Australian experience? We do not actually have any statistics, and we have not in fact moved to a simplified licensing regime yet. But one of the studies that I was involved in, the Queensland government's stage two report on the government information licensing framework, actually looked specifically at this licensing issue and at the complexities of traditional licensing. One of the participants in that study was a long-term government lawyer who had assisted in doing the simplified version of the government licenses about ten years ago, so he really knew the whole history. It is obvious: You must have something that is standardized and readily available so that you are not having to actually negotiate and draft a license on every occasion of access of this sort or where reuse is required. Without standard licenses it going to be a very expensive process. What we have been looking at, although it has not yet been implemented, is beginning some projects that adopt what we call "open content licensing." There is a lot of support in Australia at the state and federal levels for this approach.

We scoured the world for the best practice we could find. We are aware of the OPSI click-use license. What we would prefer, however, is an approach where the licensing terms are made available with the information product as it is made available. So in Australia we have a preference for something like the Creative Commons license. Now what we use might not be precisely the Creative Commons license that is used elsewhere, and if so we might have to reinvent something that essentially does the same thing as Creative Commons.

So the default position in Australia now is to use the Creative Commons attribution license and maybe, in some situations, the Creative Commons attribution and non-commercial use license. If we find that there are difficulties with that, we will probably draft a specific Creative Commons-like government license. But we want something that is interoperable within the federal government system. We are a country of only 20 million people. We cannot reinvent the wheel every time we look around, which is the tendency. So we want something that will operate not only throughout all the

Australian states and territories, but that would be consistent with concepts and licensing practices internationally.

So, basically, at this stage in Australia we are on the brink of some projects being implemented that would use such licenses. Although no study has been done to see whether it is actually cost effective, we know from practice that it is going to be more cost effective than what has prevailed to date.

PARTICIPANT: In my presentation this afternoon I will touch upon Creative Commons licensing as well. I will give you an example of one Dutch agency using one, so I can explore that issue a bit more.

PARTICIPANT: I have one suggestion for our Norwegian colleagues. It would be interesting to find out what the savings have been in the management of the geographical information (GI) in which all public bodies pooled their resources. Correct me if I am wrong, but my understanding is that because of the way that the GI is published, there is no license required between governments, and anybody in the public services can reuse the shared data and information.

So it would be very interesting to find out what the management costs savings have been from both sides, that is, both from the geographical mapping agency and also from other government bodies that do not have to enter into any sort of licensing mechanisms. That could provide some hard evidence that could be used to change some of these policies for the better.

PARTICIPANT: I wanted to speak about two things. The first is about Dr. Fornefeld's presentation on the value chain of PSI, particularly the data producers and the service providers of meteorological or geospatial information with a natural monopoly. There is no debate about the fact that there is a public need for this type of information. It is because this information is important that it is created. The data producer needs to be publicly funded because the market itself will not be able to pay for satellites, and it will not be able to pay for the experts who are able to establish maps and cartographical data. We spoke about weather information, where there can be a question as to whether or not this is a natural monopoly, but in most cases there is a natural monopoly for the public sector to produce data and then to produce a service. We see that public services have a lot of difficulties in, for example, providing new distribution platforms for this information and new kinds of services and then coming up with innovations in the services to be provided with this information.

I think there is value in distinguishing between data providers who are a natural monopoly—and who thus need public financing—and service providers. For service providers maybe there is not a natural monopoly. Perhaps public services should limit themselves to data production and provision and rely upon outside service providers who are able to do that work better. By this I do not mean that all the PSI produced should go to private organizations that will bring it to the commercial sector. Some of the information produced can be used directly from the source and not through service providers.

My second point concerns financing. It is clear that somebody has to pay for the data. The question is, Does the taxpayer have to pay for the production of data? We say that the production itself costs a lot and brings little. Production of the data is the basis of everything, but when there are no sellers, nothing is done with the data. In itself the data brings only a little return. So it has to be paid for. Who will pay for it? Are the taxpayers going to pay for it, or are the users going to pay for it?

In this debate I really have a lot of respect and admiration for the American approach. It is also clear, due to its historical heritage, that the United States is based on the circulation of information. That is not the case in Europe, at least up to now. So in Europe there is a debate: Who has to pay for the data? Is it the taxpayer, or is it the user?

We heard this morning about the cost of the licensing, the cost to buyers for the distribution of the data. I really agree that this is a cost, but it also is a potential benefit because if the data are free there is no longer a link between the data provider and the service provider. Having a business relationship between the data provider and the service provider encourages both sides to provide something that is usable.

Let me give you an example. If all the data are free, then the reusers have no leverage to ask the provider to improve the data. If the reuser partly finances the production of data, then the reuser has a right to say something to the producer of the data about the quality, because they are bearing part of the cost. This negotiation has a cost, but it is also a way to bring together the data producers and service providers so that they can work together.

PART TWO

6. Public Sector Information: Why Bother?[1]

Robbin te Velde
Dialogic, The Netherlands

I have posed the question "Why bother?" so you are already warned about the tone of this presentation. I have been involved in studying this topic for a while, and I am a bit chastened by it, but just to put it into perspective, there have been other studies before and after, and there will be more studies in the future, so it is good to compare. One may start with the Pira study in 2000,[2] which was popularized by Peter Weiss (see his "Borders in Cyberspace" at http://www.epsiplus.net/report/borders_in_cyberspace). A year later, in 2001, there was a study by the Dutch government. At that time the Dutch government supported the open access stream. They did a really good quantitative study on the value of geo-information, but they have lost much of the study's effect ever since that time. More recently, the Office of Fair Trading in the United Kingdom also published a fine study.

In terms of methods, what Pira did—and what most of the other studies have done—was to talk to some firms and then generalize the results. That is actually the way to go, in my view. It is sensible to go directly to the users because there are no standard methods available yet.

The MEPSIR[3] study was a little different. That study focused more on transparency and accessibility, on a massive pan-European scale. People were asked directly about the size of the market, what their roles were in it, and so on. One of the problems was that many people just did not know. They had no clue about PSI whatsoever, so this was clearly an immature market. In this situation, the only way to get some hard data is to go directly to the firms, but it is just not feasible to do this on a large scale—and the generalizations remain problematic.

Again, Pira started it all. The reason why we are here today is because Pira said the United States has twice the investment value for PSI, but they earn 40 times more from it. Why? The answer is that in the United States you have an open access model, and in the European Union you have a cost recovery model. This was the argument brought forward by, for instance, Peter Weiss. Although I believe the argument itself is still valid, the figures used by Pira were rather doubtful. Look, for example, at the added value of PSI quoted for the United States: a staggering $750 billion (against €68 billion for the European Union). That is almost 8 percent of U.S. gross domestic product (GDP). These are massive numbers. I think fighting in Iraq costs the United States $100 billion a year, so you can fight another 7-8 years for the same amount of money. Regardless, the

---

[1] Based on a presentation found at http://www.oecd.org/dataoecd/12/49/40064800.pdf
[2] Commission of the European Communities, 30 October 2000. *Commercial exploitation of Europe's public sector information: Final Report for the European Commission Directorate General for the Information Society.* Pira International. ftp://ftp.cordis.lu/econtent/docs/2000-1558.pdf
[3] http://www.epsiplus.net/reports/mepsir_measuring_european_public_sector_resources_report

creative bookkeeping that the study did (very successfully) raised the interest of the European Commission in PSI—and especially its potential value.

Nearly five years later, we did the MEPSIR study. You would expect that the value would be higher by that time, because even with a modest growth of 3 percent, the EU's €68 billion would now be €80 billion, but we actually arrived at a lower number, a base number of €27 billion. To be honest, that was still pretty much an overestimate. One of the things we asked for was the market size, which is different from the value added and much larger. Because all the studies had used estimates of value added, it was important in this study to use it as well in order to make comparisons.

Another issue was that it seemed the small countries tended to overestimate the value of the market significantly. Compensating for that, we divided the numbers by two. Finally, in order to fill in the missing values, we had to correct the method used. Just as Pira had done, we had used GDP as a base. But that really does not make sense because you are dealing with some big countries, such as Poland, that just do not have a vibrant information industry. So it is probably better to use the economic value of the publishing industry as a distributor of PSI, and if you do that, you arrive at lower numbers again. When we make all of these corrections, we drop from €27 to €5 billion or even €3 billion—truly a big difference. Obviously, these are not precise numbers, but they give us an order of magnitude—about 15 to 20 times less than the Pira study estimated.

Now let us look at the more recent OFT study, which covered only the United Kingdom. It arrived at an overall number of almost £600 million. If you take away all the distortions—due to trading tricks and so on—you arrive at a value of £1.1 billion, or almost double the original figure. If you then use this method to calculate a value for the European Union as a whole, you arrive at a total of €3 to €5.5 billion—pretty close to the MEPSIR figures.

Finally, let us return to the initial 2001 Dutch study. It was rather detailed, but it was focused only on geo-information and covered only the Netherlands. Extending this to all PSI sectors for all of the European Union is, of course, a very tricky business, but if you do so you end up with values of between €5 to €7 billion. Again, that is much lower than the €68 billion that was mentioned by Pira. If we take a new look at Pira, it basically said that the United States has a much stronger private information industry. Furthermore, Pira's number included IT software, hardware, Hollywood—you name it, they added everything up. But that begs the question—and this is really the key question—of to what extent this difference is due to differences in pricing policy, that is, to the difference between an open access model and a closed access model. The assumption was that there would be a more vibrant information sector if PSI were more readily available.

It is actually possible to argue the other way around. Because the United States has a much stronger private information industry, there is more of a mature demand for PSI. And there may another factor: that Americans are just better at exploiting information services, whether in the private or public sector. Or there may be no relationship whatsoever. Honestly, I do not know, and there been no research in this specific area. Gerhard Wagner from Austria is probably one of the few who has done in-depth empirical research making comparisons between countries. He has found some differences between countries in Eastern Europe, for instance. Thus, at the least we can say that there does not seem to be one single model for research.

Before 2000 (i.e., before the first generation of studies), few people were aware of the value of PSI. In many countries it was locked inside the government. So the really nice added value of the whole PSI debate is that it has opened up PSI resources. Currently, in what we can refer to as the second generation of studies, the focus is on the private sector. The basic argument is that if you simply open up PSI, you will generate a lot of money. However, what is lacking in the second generation of studies, with their exclusive focus on commercial reuse, is the broader societal value of PSI. I have been arguing this from the very start to the European Commission. Unfortunately, it is a tough sell because the hard (albeit modest) figures are in the commercial reuse area and the much bigger (yet softer) numbers in the societal use area are quite difficult to measure.

The current obsession with making money out of PSI is rather shortsighted and probably even damaging. What you see in practice, for instance, is that private sector reusers are now being squeezed from both sides. The public sector is doing some interesting things, such as giving away its information freely, and the private sector has its own goods that it makes available freely, such as open source software. So the market for private sector resusers of PSI may be getting smaller. This does not mean, however, that PSI is not relevant at all; we are just looking in the wrong places for value. It also means that we must change the way we measure value.

Up to now we have been trying to add all the individual revenues from all these firms, and even when you add everything up, you still arrive at disappointingly low numbers. I suggest that we change the perspective and look at the cost of not giving it away to the civil society. Although this may appear strange at first sight, it is already common practice in other economic domains. A prime example here is in environmental economics. There is no directive on the reuse of water, but if you would calculate what the cost is of not having clean water or not having clean air, you would arrive at massive numbers. This is how they managed to get the Clean Air Act passed in the United States.

Thus if we talk about the economic value of PSI, we should focus not only on the financial value—which is the narrow economic point of view—but also on the broader economic value. I will mention some basic methods of how to do this, which are again derived from environmental economics.

First, do not look just at the use value, but also include the non-use value. This is the value of keeping options open—for instance, of not having a database licensed exclusively to a publisher.

Second, when looking at the use value of PSI, also consider the indirect value. In the Netherlands we have the website http://www.buienradar.nl, which, translated, means "shower radar.nl." It gives low-resolution but near-real-time images of shower clouds moving over the Netherlands. We have lots of showers in the Netherlands. We also have many cyclists. Cycling in the rain is no fun. Therefore it is nice to know where the clouds are heading, so you know that you will not get wet when you cycle home. The website is a massive success. It has millions of hits each day, and this information is free. The website has the information—the low-quality radar images—free from the National Meteorological Office. The other commercial weather bureaus did not care about this information because the images were of such low quality. Buienradar.nl, however, put the information free on the Internet and generated income from advertisements. The revenues from advertisements are a direct economic proxy, but the broader economic impacts are much bigger. You may measure these impacts, for instance, by asking people what is it worth to them that they do not get wet when riding home on their bicycles. It is not really quite that simple. You have to be rather specific in describing what the services are that may be derived from a particular piece of PSI, but there is already a lot of experience with estimating this kind of hedonistic pricing. As a first attempt, I would guess the overall benefits of making PSI freely available to society are around the original Pira figures for Europe, i.e., €60-€70 billion.

So why bother? Actually, this is exactly what I said one and a half years ago, here in Paris: (1) Government is a major producer of information, and (2) there is a lot of money involved in the commercial exploitation of information.

It appears that there is a huge (potential) pot of gold, which is currently the second-generation view. However, it is important to keep in mind that (1) and (2) are separate things. Public sector information is important in its own right. If you think it is important, then use taxpayers' money to produce it, and do not mix it up with private use. If you want a dynamic private European information industry, then you will need to take various steps, such as doing something about competition policies. But this has nothing to do with PSI, per se.

How then does one determine the overall total economic value of PSI—including its wider societal value? This depends, really, upon the view of the citizen. If citizens think it is important, then the government should spend tax money on it. I want to emphasize that we should also take this wider (and important) societal value into account; only then will we be able to arrive at some hard numbers, following the methods in studying environmental economics as an example. One should not, however, focus too much on the value of commercial reuse. That is not the huge pot of gold after all, and to focus exclusively on it may even work against getting the most economic value out of PSI.

7. Measuring the Economic Impact of the PSI Directive in the Context of the 2008 Review[1]

Chris Corbin
ePSI*plus*, United Kingdom

This presentation will cover the period from July 1, 2005, when the European Union's (EU) directive on the re-use of public sector information[2] came into force within member states, until the time of the EU's review in 2008. The ePSI*plus* project is a thematic network. Its purpose is to support the directive by helping potential users understand the opportunities associated with PSI use and reuse. The network is planned to be operational for 30 months, from September 2006 through the end of February 2009, with a relatively minimal total budget of €950,000, and it will cover the 33 countries of the European Union and the European Free Trade Area. The project is concerned with all aspects of PSI, even those that are excluded from the directive, and it is intended to serve every type of stakeholder. Under the rules of the EU eContent*plus* Program for thematic networks, participation of the network partners is voluntary. The audience includes more than 50 million public servants in Europe, employed at several million public sector bodies, plus an unknown number of potential private sector reusers; these numbers are constantly changing as the public and private sectors are reconfigured.

The project's strategy is to gather evidence and monitor the value chain, beginning with the PSI directive and then observing how that transfers into government policy within a country, how this policy is actually interpreted by the PSI holder, and then how the policy is interpreted by the reuser, either commercial or noncommercial. There clearly is a gap between the policy maker and the PSI holder, and attention must be given to improving the way that policy makers actually monitor the effectiveness of their policies. This is difficult, however, because of the large and diverse number of policy makers in Europe. A second gap arises from the resistance factor that favors protectionist policies and practices; it is important to quantify the results of this resistance. There is a general perception that regulators are underfunded, but this has to be quantified in order to justify more funds. Yet another issue is that in Europe, where so much commerce takes place across borders, it will be important in monitoring PSI reuse to look at single market areas rather than individual countries.

Defining "reuse" is quite a large topic, and one of the challenges of this topic is that most reuse of PSI starts with small companies that have only one or a few employees. Another difficulty is monitoring legal cases in which a particular reuse is challenged. Legal issues are not easy to understand and can vary based on the EU member state, but an analysis of them generally shows that member states are not doing particularly well in implementing even the basic parts of the directive, the main goal of

---

[1] Based on a presentation found at http://www.oecd.org/dataoecd/12/48/40064809.pdf
[2] Commission of the European Communities. 2003. *Directive 2003/9 8/EC of Parliament and Council on the re-use of public sector information.* Found at
http://ec.europa.eu/information_society/policy/psi/docs/pdfs/directive/psi_directive_en.pdf

which is simplification. It is remarkable how, because of the normal human tendency of making things complex, that goal has been lost as one goes down the value chain.

So is the ePSI*plus* thematic network working? In answering that question, it is important to keep in mind several facts. First, there are various constraints involved in any network, such as ePSI*plus*, where participation is voluntary. Second, any project that operates across Europe is quite challenging because it faces a multilingual and multicultural environment. Third, the markets are all at different stages of development, each with a huge range of PSI stakeholders and competition. The public sector is competing with the private sector, and private sector entities are competing with each other. Business strategy and information are generally considered proprietary by the PSI holders.

Furthermore, there is a lack of measurement tools, especially for economic modeling and understanding data apart from the macro level. One key issue is: When the pendulum swings from high charges for obtaining PSI to being free of charge, how is the public task maintained and how much money is involved? If the pendulum suddenly swings, how many companies that have relied on the current model are likely to go out of business? And how is the new model charted over time? While it has been possible to analyze the legal issues, it is more difficult to analyze the economic and social effects. Since this information comes from the people involved in the PSI-related activities, it has been critical to develop better relationships with those in the field.

The project is also looking at trends in order to identify good practices and to determine what can be replicated across member states. For example, if a country has a complaints procedure that is dedicated to reuse, how does it compare with a country that does not have one? What is the effect of having a complaints procedure, and does it result in a measurable difference between the countries? Since the project is only at its midlife, determining the effect of any activity is not easy. The number of PSI stakeholders becoming interested in these topics is definitely growing, however, and it is clear that the presence of the directive has forced the pace of the debate.

So what has been the impact of the PSI directive? The understanding of and expertise with PSI is low, and that is the real issue. People understand basics, but what is still lacking is a real understanding of the complexity of PSI in terms of how it relates to governance, how governments change, and how that affects PSI activities. There is no straightforward answer, either in the European context or the global context. Part of the problem is that there are few among the EU member states who actually see PSI as an economic factor, even though a chief focus of the Lisbon Treaty is to develop the knowledge economy. Unfortunately, policy makers often do not think outside of their own country, and they do not see why they should be thinking beyond it.

Finally, there remains a huge challenge in addressing the educational needs about PSI and disentangling what people say from what they believe. People can remember what the situation was like pre-2003, before the PSI directive was finalized, but that is not all that helpful. As the ePSI*plus* project holds more meetings and the attendance grows, each meeting needs to move forward on what the issues are today and to stop harping on what went on in the past. Nevertheless, the network process is slowly working, and that is a hopeful sign for more success in the future.

8. Different PSI Access Policies and Their Impact[1]

Frederika Welle Donker
Delft University of Technology, The Netherlands

I work for the GeoPortal Network Project in the Netherlands. In the Netherlands, there is a large research program called Ruimte voor Geo-Informatie (RGI), or the Space for Geo Information Program, and the government has spent about €20 million on it over a five-year period. The GeoPortal Network (GPN) Project is one of the activities under the RGI Program. The objective of the project is to set up one-stop shop for all geo information. The GPN Project is run by a consortium of 14 partners from both the public and private sectors. My research is to identify the current legal and financial barriers to access and to develop a model for transparent access. The goal of this model, called the Backx model, is to develop a system in which different data can be combined without running into various types of barriers. This can be a problem because quite often one organization will comply but not the other. The model should be suitable for all types of reusers, whether from the private sector, the public sector, or the end users themselves.

There are three levels of accessibility in the Backx model. First, information has to be known. If no one knows about the information, if they cannot find it, if they cannot recognize it, then it is of no use at all. Second, once someone knows it is there, they have to be allowed to get it. It has to be affordable. Third—and this is the responsibility of whoever creates the data—the quality of the data has to be good enough. The data must be clear, manageable, and usable. The GeoPortal Network Project is not going to examine the quality of the data, but instead it will focus on where the data can be found and how they can be used.

What is geo information (GI)? It is all information that refers to a specific location on Earth. We are concerned with GI in the public sector domain. In the Netherlands, public-sector geo information is available for reuse under certain conditions. There are two regimes used for dissemination: the marginal-costs regime and the cost-recovery regime. The type of regime used depends on the type of government agency and what its financial base is.

How is geo information different from other types of information? It is not based on text. It is not like digitizing legislation and making it available through a PDF file. While that takes time, it is relatively easy. Geo information typically is based on very specific data sets, which can be very expensive to collect and maintain. They are also subject to intellectual property rights as well as to national security and privacy laws, so before GI is made available for use or reuse, the data sets may have to be prepared for public dissemination. That is one of the reasons why reuse is often covered by licenses. The licenses are not only to protect intellectual property rights but also to comply with security and privacy laws. The licenses also allow cost recovery. Nonetheless, geo information has unlimited potential applications for the private sector.

---

[1] Based on a presentation found at http://www.oecd.org/dataoecd/12/36/40066090.pdf

European Union directives related to GI include the PSI directive on the re-use of public sector information and the INSPIRE directive.[2] What is the difference? They overlap to a certain extent, but the PSI directive focuses on reuse of public sector information, while the INSPIRE directive focuses on sharing GI with the public sector. INSPIRE stipulates which standards to use for exchanging and sharing data, but neither of these directives regulates market activities. Although both stipulate a preference for a marginal-costs pricing regime, EU member states are still allowed to use the cost-recovery regime.

The Dutch legislation governing the use and reuse of geo information is the Wet openbaarheid van bestuur, which is generally equivalent to the American Freedom of Information Act. There is also contract law that comes into play in some situations. In the Netherlands public sector organizations are excluded from fair trade legislation, but that is currently under review. There is protection-of-privacy legislation as well, which states that if there is any information that can be traced directly back to a person, then it is not allowed for reuse. Finally, there is specific legislation such as the Cadastre Act, discussed in more detail below.

Up until the mid-1990s, public sector organizations could set their own conditions and prices for marketing PSI. They could market it themselves, or they could give it away, but the latter was not a common approach. The private sector complained vociferously about unfair trading practices. This resulted in a report[3] that made a number of sweeping recommendations. One recommendation was that public sector organizations should not engage in market activity in competition with the private sector. The Cohen report listed a number of exceptions having to do with core tasks, however. One exception was that while public sector organizations should not be allowed to add value to their own information with the goal of making the information more attractive for reselling it; they should be permitted to add value if this is required in order to fulfill their essential mission.

Another recommendation in the report was that the marketing activities of several public sector organizations should be reviewed. For example, the National Meteorology Office and the Cadastre were reviewed. The result was that a number of these organizations were privatized outright, while others, like the Met Office, had to give up their commercial arms. If they were going to sell their data for reuse, they had to do it through an intermediary, in order to create a level playing field with a full-cost recovery regime.

The report also published guidelines for national public sector bodies that are not covered by their own specific legislation. The guidelines stated that if a public sector organization were to engage in economic activities because the private sector would not or could not, then all costs must be passed on in the charges. Basically, a public sector body was not allowed to give its data away free, because if it did, it would be competing unfairly with the private sector. So, if there were to be competition, it would be on a level

---

[2] Commission of the European Communities. 2007. *Directive 2007/2/EC of the European Parliament and of the Council of 14 March 2007 establishing an Infrastructure for Spatial Information in the European Community.* Found at http://inspire.jrc.ec.europa.eu/

[3] *Markt en Overheid* (Market Functioning, Deregulation and Quality of Legislation). 1998. 'Eindrapport' van de MDW-werkgroep (commissie Cohen). Ministerie van Economische Zaken: Den Haag.

playing field, and the public sector body was not allowed to use cross-subsidies or tax advantages.

Unfortunately, these guidelines do not apply to lower levels of government, such as municipalities, provinces, or water boards. They only apply to the national public sector, even though most of the original complaints from the private sector did not apply to the national public sector, but rather to the lower levels because they were the ones setting their own charges and license conditions.

So what is happening now? The public sector is not supposed to be producing value-added products, except those entities specifically mandated to do so. This is a very elastic concept, however, and there are no clear boundaries. The national Cadastre, which is covered by its own legislation, is an exception, as it is producing value-added products in direct competition with the private sector. Otherwise, more and more public sector data sets are becoming available for reuse thanks to the PSI directive, although there is still great variety in licensing conditions. I did a quick overview about two years ago, and the licenses of the 20 or so public sector bodies that I looked at ranged from a license that was just one or two paragraphs to a license that was extremely complex. Also, to negotiate a license can demand anything from a click-through license to actually having to go through many weeks of negotiations. The resulting situation is not transparent, and it can be very time consuming.

Among the more attractive data sets are the Authentic Registries.[4] The private sector really would like to have these data because they can be used for value adding. The Authentic Registries are still restricted for reuse, and they are not made public. The concept behind the Authentic Registries is that governments should acquire information only once and should reuse it many times, which implies that there should be only one registry for the entire population. There is only one registry for cars, for example, and only one Cadastral registry. All other public sector bodies are to reuse that same registry. If they see any mistakes they are supposed to report them to the responsible body so they can be fixed. The goal is for the registries to be of very high quality. The registries are very valuable for the private sector. Private companies would especially like to have the property value register, which allows one to see how much houses are worth. But the Authentic Registeries are not available for use, let alone reuse.[2]

Prices of PSI are coming down. It is a major trend. Some of them are coming down because the organizations have decided to make their PSI available for only the cost of dissemination, but many of them are coming down because the prices were too

---

[4] An authentic register is defined in the Netherlands' Streamlining Key Data Programme as 'a high quality database accompanied by explicit guarantees ensuring for its quality assurance that, in view of the entirety of statutoryduties, contains essential and/or frequently-used data pertaining to persons, institutions, issues, activities or occurrences and which is designated by law as the sole officially recognised register of the relevant data to be used by all government agencies and, if possible, by private organisations throughout the entire country, unless important reasons such as the protection of privacy explicitly preclude the use of the register'. Duivenbode, H van & M de Vries. 2003, *Upstream! A chronicle of the Streamlining Key Data Programme.* The Hague.

[5] At the time of the presentation, legislation related to the Authentic Registries was not finalised. Since then the legislation process has moved forward. It now looks as though reuse of the Authentic Registries will be allowed (i.e., not restricted due to proprietary concerns, or security or privacy legislation). The pricing regime has not been finalised yet, however.

high and the organizations did not sell any data sets. For example, there is a data set which records all the geographic heights in the Netherlands. You may laugh because our highest mountain is only 100 meters, but it is actually quite important for the lower-lying areas to see how much below sea level they are, or for use in the three-dimensional imaging of buildings. The price used to be €1 million for a set covering the entire country. I think they sold one. Now the price has been reduced to €200,000, and about 20 have been sold. This shows that lowering prices actually can increase revenue.

The problem now is that if you are giving free data away to the public sector, this may be deemed to be economic activity. The positive side is we get the stimulation of the knowledge economy and more value-added products, which also means more taxes flowing back to the government, because if we are going to get more companies producing value-added products there is going to be more revenue flowing back to the government in the form of sales taxes, value added taxes, company taxes, and income taxes from the new employees. Ultimately, the government will get a better return on investment, but it is a long-term strategy and most governments only look ahead as far as the next election and don't look beyond that point.

Another positive effect of this activity is the encouragement of citizen involvement. Citizens now have better access to information and are better informed. This gets us back to the issue of how much it is worth: How much does it cost if you do not have the information? There is no such thing as a free lunch. If you do not expend the resources, the ability to sustain the quality of data is threatened. The Dutch Cadastre is an example. It used to be funded out of general revenue, but during the 1990s the budget was cut many times. It almost ceased to exist because it was not getting enough money to maintain a Cadastre register.

As part of the Cohen report the Dutch Cadastre was reviewed, reorganized, and turned into what the English would call a Trading Fund. It is doing very well now, and it does not want to go back to the former situation in which it was depending on an annual budget and hoping that it would have enough money to survive.

Another downside of making the PSI available at low cost or no cost is the threat to the private sector companies that may have already set up similar data sets. If the public sector is going to make these data sets available free of charge, then it will be seen as an unfair trading practice, and the private sector will have unrecoverable costs.

I have to make some mention of the Creative Commons.[5] Creative Commons is a nonprofit organization founded in the United States using a "some-rights-reserved" approach, in contrast to the "all-rights-reserved" approach of the copyright law. Creative Commons has developed a number of standard licenses and simplified mechanisms for using them. If you want to select a license, you do it online and answer a few questions.

The information to which a Creative Commons license can be applied can be any copyrighted work, as long as it is in digital format. It can be a document, a photograph, a map, or any other copyrighted work. There are six Creative Commons licenses: Attribution, Attribution Share Alike, Attribution No Derivatives, Attribution Non-Commercial, Attribution Non-Commercial Share Alike, and Attribution Non-

---

[6] http://creativecommons.org/

Commercial No Derivatives. The licenses are valid for the whole duration of copyright. Each license appears in three versions because not everyone is a lawyer. Each Creative Commons license first appears in a layman's version, which uses a symbol and a few very short lines that can be easily understood. It is all on one page. After the layman's version is a legal version. In the Netherlands the Creative Commons license has been upheld by the court, so it is tested as legally binding. In addition to the layman's and legal versions, there is also a machine readable version, which is very useful if you want to make information findable to those using a search engine online. This makes it possible to restrict a search, for example, to all the information that can be used for commercial purposes. The search will retrieve every Creative Commons licensed product in that category.

One case study is of the New Map of the Netherlands, which is managed by an organization called the Department of Housing and Special Planning. The data set contains all planning information as a GIS file. It used to be available through an intermediary, and the intermediary sold 20 sets in 20 months' time. For that data set this is not cost effective. Instead, the department decided to make the set downloadable with the Creative Commons "attribution only" license and to see what would happen. The result is there are now about 200 downloads per month. However, the department still has to pay license fees to the Cadastre for the use of the topographic map as an underground layer. This is a case of one agency paying money to another government agency, which is very inefficient.

The other case study is of the National Roads Dataset managed by the Department of Public Works. This consists of information that is collected in collaboration with other public sector bodies, and it contains a great deal of other data having to do with roads, such as maintenance data. It has many attributes, but it is not the data concerning the roads that people want. What they usually want is the collection of various attributes, such as street numbering, that would cost a lot of money if they were to be purchased as a separate file from another organization. The private sector sets up similar data sets, and Dr. Fornefeld already mentioned Tele Atlas and Navteq. The Department of Public Works wants to make the National Roads Dataset available, and it is already available to use freely now. The department intends to make it available for reuse beginning next year. This has resulted in questions in parliament and threats of litigation.[3] It is a mess.

But what is happening in the meantime? We have organizations like Google Earth getting the data from whoever has it, in the private sector or the public sector. Google Earth provides free reference data and allows mash-ups. Even public sector organizations in the Netherlands are considering using Google Earth rather than the data from the Cadastre because the Cadastre charges for the data, while Google Earth does not, or at

---

[7]Since then, the National Roads Dataset has been withdrawn from viewing by the Department of Public Works. The complaints by organizations selling the street numbering file attributes in question were not upheld. However, the complaints by Falkplan Andes, a cartography company, about unfair trading practices were upheld. Falkplan Andes claimed that making the National Roads Dataset available for free would spoil the market for commercial cartographers. Because these private firms had already invested in similar datasets, their investments could not be recouped any longer. It is not known if the Department of Public Works will make the dataset available in the next couple of years or what will happen to the copies supplied under the Freedom of Information Act before the dataset was withdrawn.

least the price is negotiable. The public just wants free services. If the members of the public cannot get free information from the government, they will try to get it from somewhere else.

In conclusion, the accessibility is improving, but the municipalities also need to comply with the Freedom of Information Act. There is still too much emphasis on protecting intellectual property rights. There are still no consistent and transparent licenses, although the government agencies are trying to work on that. Transparency of cost is needed too, as is some legal clarification about what is an economic activity under the law. There are some court cases pending, and until they are resolved, there will be no clarity.

Here are my recommendations: Simplify current licenses and guarantee the funding. If an agency is going to make GI available free of charge, it should be funded from the current budget. At this time such information cannot be funded from sales alone so, yes, perhaps we should involve the private sector.

Within the GeoPortal Consortium we are working with both the public and private sectors, and the private sector really enjoys it. If they can get something out of it like free data, they will help you develop services. For the Authentic Registries, the current legislation is insufficient. The public sector activity will be overtaken by services such as Google Earth's, and in five years' time the opportunity will be lost.

9. The Price of Everything but the Value of Nothing[1]

Antoinette Graves
Office of Fair Trading, United Kingdom

Oscar Wilde defined a cynic as someone who knows the price of everything but the value of nothing, which is apt for understanding PSI and ultimately what is being done to promote PSI access and reuse policies. Policy makers wish to maximize the value of PSI to the economy as a whole, but when public sector bodies charge for PSI, those costs can actually inhibit others from adding value. The same is true with licensing restrictions even if they are put in place to protect the bodies that want to exploit the data and set their own prices.

When the Office of Fair Trading (OFT) carried out its study on public sector information, the purpose was to examine whether the market was working well for end consumers, defined more broadly than just citizens or taxpayers. To answer whether the market was working well, the intention was to look beyond competition for competition's sake and, in particular, to look further up the supply chain to determine whether the market was working well between public sector bodies and businesses and among the public sector bodies themselves, and then to make suggestions that took into account the size and the potential size of the market.

At the risk of sounding like a character in *Alice in Wonderland*, the answer of how to measure the value of PSI is that it all depends on what you want to know. To begin, OFT needed an estimate of the current value and size of the market. It was then necessary to determine the current income to PSI holders as well as the value to the businesses that are using and reusing the information, but without double counting. To determine the former, OFT had access to some reasonably reliable figures, but for the latter new economic modeling had to be done.

Not surprisingly, OFT concluded that public sector information is valuable and vitally important for businesses. There were a lot of products that just could not be made, or that could not be made in the form that they were, without access to and reuse of public sector information. When problems arose it was often due to public sector bodies that were in some way adding value themselves. In addition to gathering the information at the upstream level, these bodies were doing something downstream that gave them an incentive to restrict access to the upstream level. Thus it was important to identify the monopoly element in order to begin solving some of the problems. For example, it was determined that marginal-cost pricing is not necessarily the answer. While public sector bodies may use differential pricing and recover more of their costs on certain products or users than on others, they may still restrict what is available. Moreover, when value is added, if a marginal price is charged, it is undercutting the competition.

The maximum that should be charged for the monopoly (or upstream) would be full cost recovery—plus, in the United Kingdom, the required rate of return to the Treasury. At the same time, if the public sector is doing something with the PSI that the

---

[1] Based on a presentation found at http://www.oecd.org/dataoecd/12/34/40066135.pdf

private sector could also do if it had access to the upstream information, then that qualifies as a downstream activity and the minimum amount charged should be full cost recovery, because anything less would be undercutting competition. It is not necessarily possible to ban public sector bodies from the downstream market altogether and, in some cases, there could be some genuine economies of scale or scope because of vertically integrated public sector bodies that have the capabilities to perform downstream activities. The main concern is to ensure a level playing field so that competition can occur, and if the private sector can make downstream products more cheaply or meet consumer demands in other ways, then the public sector body should consider pulling out of the market.

One implication of these considerations is that public sector bodies should make their information available at the earliest point that it is useful to businesses. The public entities should not complicate things by bundling their information with other data and then not allowing the private sector access to the background data. While it may be necessary to have aggregated and anonymous provision of personal data at the first stage, when it is still upstream data, the data should be made available on the same basis as to the entities' own downstream operations—that is, for the same pricing and licensing terms.

In terms of assessing the value of PSI, there are improvements that could lead to a doubling in the value of PSI to around a billion pounds per year. How is this possible? Whereas previous studies have looked at the gross value added by PSI to the economy—a top-down approach—the tendency was for these studies to overestimate the real value of PSI to the economy because they were not looking at any possible substitutes. For example, the Pira study in 2000 used the turnover of public sector bodies, and that figure included non-PSI-related income, government grants, and so on. Other studies, such as the Ordnance Survey commissioned in 1999, also used this top-down approach. The contribution of Ordnance Survey data to Great Britain was estimated to be between £79 billion and £136 billion, representing about 12 to 20 percent of the gross value added to the entire economy during 1996. Roger Timm and Partners conducted a top-down study for the British Geological Survey (BGS), assessing its value at 8 percent of GDP, or £34 billion to £61 billion. These numbers clearly overstate the significance of these organizations, because to conclude that together they underpin over 25 percent of the economic activity in the United Kingdom is just not plausible. It would not take many more studies before the conclusion would be that PSI contributed 100 percent or more of the economic activity in the United Kingdom. Thus, the top-down approach ignores the counterfactual, because it ignores what happens in the absence of PSI.

It is better to look at the value of PSI today in terms of net economic value by estimating the willingness to pay for PSI minus the cost of producing and supplying it—that is, a bottom-up approach. To that end, OFT looked at the consumer detriment, the types of detriment that could occur, and the likelihood of them occurring for any given group of PSI holders, as well as the potential magnitude of each negative factor. The types of detriment included: unduly high pricing; restriction of downstream competition, including refusal to supply or discrimination; and failure to exploit PSI. The income of PSI holders was examined by asking how much they earned directly from their information activity, excluding government grants, and, especially, if other public sector bodies were customers. The resulting calculation indicated that the net value of public sector information in the United Kingdom is about 590 million pounds per year. The costs of the three types of detriments were estimated to be £20 million from high pricing, £140 million from restriction of downstream competition, and £360 million from failure to exploit PSI. Thus OFT suggests that the net value of public sector information in the United Kingdom could be increased to approximately £1.1 billion pounds by resolving all of the problems already identified.

The reactions to the OFT study were interesting. Clearly, the bottom-up approach is more accurate, not least because the possibility of alternative products and services is considered. As a result, some of the public sector bodies approached OFT immediately and asked for help with their pricing policies to make sure that they were not unfairly competing or restricting competition. The British government accepted many of the study's recommendations, except the recommendation for a splitting in accounting terms of the upstream and downstream, i.e., the monopolistic and non-monopolistic elements. The Treasury has commissioned Cambridge University to do a cost-benefit analysis of whether to split the accounts and to look at different pricing models. That additional report is expected soon.

10. Enhancing Access to Government Information: Economic Theory as It Applies to Statistics Canada[1]

Kirsti Nilsen
University of Western Ontario, Canada

This presentation summarizes a study I did for Statistics Canada, that country's national statistical agency. The goals of this study were to complete an authoritative view and analysis of current economic theory, to review the literature on the economic theory of information, and to identify elements of the literature relevant to Statistics Canada's dissemination and management of the production of statistics. My focus was on several issues: the impact of information on general economic efficiency; the economic rationale for, and advantages of, public sector supply as opposed to private sector supply of information; economic theory with respect to pricing; the economic rationale for government intervention in the statistical information market; and the appropriate level of production of official statistics. I was also tasked to summarize and review Statistics Canada's production and dissemination program in light of current economic theory and to identify areas where I thought that the agency's production program could be improved.

In reviewing the literature, I first focused on economics broadly and then looked in more depth at the economics of information. While there is an abundance of theoretical literature on the economics of information, there is very little on the economics of public sector information and almost nothing on the economics of official statistical information.

It is worth noting that theoretical economists do not focus on the financial situation of individual organizations, so if an agency like Statistics Canada is efficient and claims to be making money and covering its costs, it is not their concern. These theorists work at a broader level and are concerned with the economic and social welfare of society as a whole. They look not only at economic efficiency but also at the larger questions, What is the social benefit? What is the social welfare?

The belief among economists is that economic efficiency is achieved when goods and services that are produced actually exchange hands, avoiding wasteful overproduction and fulfilling consumer wants, desires, or preferences. Conversely, it is economically inefficient if agencies or organizations produce information that does not exchange hands and if there are desires that the consumers have that could be satisfied by PSI producers but that are not being fulfilled by them.

Theoretical economists also consider externalities, or spillovers, in their analyses. They care about positive externalities, while remaining aware of the butterfly effect, which refers to the way that a very small bit of information can have large downstream impact. Furthermore, they argue that cost recovery through such mechanisms as user fees is never welfare enhancing. This conviction is repeated over and over in the literature. Economists believe instead that taxation has distributive benefits across society (cf., Joseph Stiglitz).

---

[1] Based on a presentation found at http://www.oecd.org/dataoecd/12/32/40066153.pdf

According to economists, public goods are goods that can be consumed by many without detracting from the benefits enjoyed by others. Public goods are nonrivalrous and nonexcludable. That is, their use by some consumers does not affect their availability to other consumers and no one can be excluded from using them. The classic example of a pure public good is the lighthouse, whose benefits are available to anyone and everyone. Public goods can also be produced by the private sector (which is counterintuitive to most people), with the classic example being the newspaper. While produced by the private sector, the information in a newspaper is nonrivalrous and nonexcludable. No newspaper publisher can keep me from passing on to others the information I read this morning. However, the private sector does not in general produce enough of these goods for which there is no market or sufficient revenue, and very often these are the goods with social benefits. It is this situation that underlies the justification for the public sector supply of public goods.

Some public goods can be made rivalrous and excludable, with education being a classic example. While information is almost always nonrivalrous, it may be made excludable by pricing, copyright, or failure to provide access electronically or in print.

Pricing of nonrivalrous public goods, such as information, is never economically efficient because some people will be prevented from enjoying the benefit of the good even though their consumption of the good would have little or no marginal cost to the producer. Pricing implies that information is a commodity, but information's characteristics make such a categorization problematic—information's content is easily shared, resistant to appropriation, and difficult to measure. Attempting to value information is challenging, because once information is disseminated, it can be spread around and have immense and often unanticipated downstream effects. For all of these reasons, information is difficult to cost and to price.

Moreover, wider dissemination of information does not increase the costs to the producer. This situation makes possible the monopolistic provision of information goods by those who can take full advantage of the economies of scale. (cf., Carl Shapiro and Hal Varian). Economists recognize that private sector monopolists underproduce and overprice their goods and that public sector information producers are usually monopolists. Economists also argue that pricing above the marginal cost of dissemination is inefficient because it results in a deadweight loss and eliminates the consumer surplus. Consumer surplus can be thought of as money left over because a good cost less than expected: If a person has set aside $50 to buy a shirt, and the shirt is actually bought on sale for $25, the consumer surplus is $25. Consumer surplus is economically efficient because consumers will generally take that $25 and do something else with it that is good for the economy. They may buy another item or invest the money. This consumer surplus is lost when prices are set above marginal cost. Furthermore, such pricing means that some items will be produced and not sold, which is economically inefficient, or else units that have benefits greater than their cost will not be purchased. Economists agree that there is no net social benefit to charging above marginal cost.

When the public sector does impose user fees for information, it claims that they are based on marginal cost or on cost recovery pricing. The question is, What is being included in the marginal cost? Some of the literature indicates there is a long-term marginal cost and a short-term marginal cost, but what is the difference? It appears that long-term marginal cost is another way of saying full cost, or cost-recovery pricing. But the problem remains: How are the costs determined? Do you include the lights? The air conditioning? The price, then, is always a political decision—and arbitrary. According to economists, there is no way to price information in an objective manner.

So why does the public sector want to impose fees? The basic answer is that it is to recover costs and generate revenue. Beginning in 1984-1985, the Canadian government imposed cost recovery and revenue generation on government agencies, and while this has been the operational model ever since, various agencies are now moving away from it (which is why Statistics Canada wanted this study done).

The justification for cost recovery is often based on the so-called benefit principle: Those who benefit from a good should pay for it. However, it is very difficult to determine the benefits of information. Information flows. It moves away from the initial buyer. So, what is the benefit? Who benefits? How do you apply the benefit principle? The assignment of benefit, like the assignment of costs, is an arbitrary exercise.

Some countries impose copyrights on PSI. This, too, must certainly have unanticipated downstream consequences. For example, what happens to countries, such as Canada, that impose Crown copyright on their information when they trade with other countries, such as the United States, that do not? Are Canadian businesses on a level playing field with American businesses in our competitive trade market? No. To be sure, the main argument for retaining copyright is that it ensures the integrity and authority of the information. Elizabeth Judge, who is a legal scholar in Canada, thinks that as a means of ensuring PSI integrity and authority, copyright is very much a blunt instrument. In Canada, for instance, the moral rights provisions of the Copyright Act are sufficient to ensure PSI integrity and authority, and it is not necessary to impose Crown copyright. The copyright acts in many countries in the European Union include moral rights provisions. Of course, the real reason that some countries retain copyright is to generate revenue on the initial information and on any value added to it. Imposing copyright allows PSI providers to benefit from adding value to their own information or from licensing others who wish to add value. Economists have concluded that Crown copyright has social costs and a negative economic impact.

Stiglitz, Orszag, and Orszag (2000) argued that if a government role is warranted in any activity, then seeking to generate revenue means that an agency is not fulfilling its mission. And if no government role is warranted, the activity should be undertaken by the private sector. Thus it is a proper government role to provide public data and information to support basic research and to improve the efficiency with which the services of government are provided.

However, Stiglitz, Orszag and Orszag also argued that PSI providers should exercise caution in adding specialized value to public data and information beyond a basic level. If there is a need for specialization, then it probably should not be done by the public sector, and the cutoff should come at the point when the marginal costs become high. Governments should leave high marginal cost activities to the private sector. Furthermore, PSI providers should only provide a service online when a private service would not be more efficient, taking into account privacy, security, and consumer protection.

In the digital economy, private markets may produce substantial income inequality and excessive investment because of attempts to become the best in a specific field, which leads to the markets becoming inefficient from a social perspective. Because of its high fixed costs and its low marginal costs, the production of information is always at risk of having limited competition. To avoid this, competition must be encouraged, which will lead to lower prices, which in turn benefits the entire society. Otherwise, given the high fixed costs and low marginal costs, it is likely that monopolies will develop.

Stiglitz, Orszag and Orszag conclude that the theoretical underpinnings of the private–versus-public situation shifts as the economy moves toward a digital one. Although it may seem to be inconsistent with the laissez-faire approach to economic efficiency, this movement toward a digital economy implies an expansion of public goods and suggests a larger public role in the digital economy.

What are the implications for PSI providers, such as Statistics Canada, of moving to free dissemination? Statistics Canada is an entrepreneurial agency whose budget benefits from the sale of its data. I understand that there is a ground shift going on, with the agency considering a move towards free (or less restricted) dissemination. While one can predict that the agency's sales and licensing revenues will decrease, it is also true that usage and reuse will increase. Increased usage would have positive externalities in terms of information dissemination and the uses to which people will put the data, and it will also have a positive economic impact for the country as a whole, ultimately leading to increased tax revenues that are generated by the use and reuse of PSI.

At the same time, the agency's transaction and opportunity costs will decrease. A great deal of money and time is currently spent determining prices, negotiating and administering licenses, and monitoring where sales revenues are coming from, who is paying, and who has not paid. Furthermore, much time and money is spent negotiating with other government departments over cost recovery charges for information, which generates a great deal of wasted transaction costs and produces no new revenues for the government as a whole. That money could be put to other uses. I conclude that the decreases in transaction and opportunity cost will more than compensate for the revenue decrease; meanwhile, there will be a positive economic impact for the country from increased use of the data and the tax revenue increases resulting from private sector reuse. Overall this outcome will result in increased economic efficiency and a greater net social benefit.

REFERENCES

Judge, E. F. 2005. Crown copyright and copyright reform in Canada. In *In the Public Interest: The Future of Canadian Copyright Law,* edited by M. Geist. Toronto: Irwin Law. Pp. 550-594.

Shapiro, C., and H. Varian. 1999. *Information Rules: A Strategic Guide to the Network Economy.* Boston: Harvard Business School Press.

Stiglitz, J. E. 1994. *Whither Socialism.* Cambridge, MA: MIT Press.

Stiglitz, J. E., P. R. Orszag, and J. M. Orszag. 2000. *The Role of Government in a Digital Age.* Washington, DC: Computer and Communications Industry Association.

11. Assessing the Impact of Public Sector Geographic Information[1]

Max Craglia
Institute for Environment and Sustainability, JRC, Italy

The Infrastructure for Spatial Information in Europe (INSPIRE) is a directive of the European Parliament and the Council (EC/2007/2) that is based on the various infrastructures for spatial information set up and operated by the EU member states. The purpose of the INSPIRE directive is to support environmental policy making and, in particular, to support the formulation, implementation, monitoring, and evaluation of environmental policies across the European Community and to overcome major barriers that affect the availability and accessibility of pertinent spatial data. The key components of the INSPIRE directive, as is true of any Spatial Data Infrastructure (SDI), include: metadata (the documentation of what information resources exist, who has responsibility for them, and how they can be accessed); technical specifications for the interoperability of spatial datasets and spatial services; network services to allow the discovery, view, download, transformation, and linkage of datasets and services; policies for sharing data and services; and complementary measures for monitoring and reporting on the implementation of the directive. The INSPIRE directive covers 34 data themes necessary to support environmental policy and includes geographic, administrative, social, and environmental information.[2] The directive came into force on May 15, 2007, and member states have until May 2009 to transpose the directive into national legislation, with implementation taking place over a 10-year period.

There is a significant degree of synergy between the INSPIRE directive and the PSI directives, as the geographic and environmental information of the INSPIRE directive represents a significant portion of the total economic value of PSI, and the data themes of INSPIRE are primarily related to issues in the public sector. There are also various differences between the two. For example, the PSI directive defines the rules for exploiting PSI once it has been made available, but it allows the EU member states the freedom to define what information they make available as well as when and how. By contrast, the INSPIRE directive is more prescriptive, and it defines clearly what information must be made available within a certain timeframe, in what format it must appear, and how it should be documented and made accessible. The INSPIRE directive therefore addresses three of the main issues surrounding PSI: discovery, availability, and use. From this perspective, the implementation of the INSPIRE directive promises to improve significantly the availability of PSI.

The INSPIRE and PSI directives share an interest in assessing the impacts of making information more widely available and used. In January 2006 the Joint Research Centre (JRC) of the European Commission organized a workshop to review best practices in the assessment of SDIs, to compare methodologies and findings and to see what lessons could be learned from similar large-scale infrastructures. Among the key findings of that workshop was that when a case has to be made to obtain funding for an SDI, the

---

[1] Based on a presentation found at http://www.oecd.org/dataoecd/32/25/40359068.pdf
[2] See http://inspire.jrc.ec.europa.eu

case is generally based on assumptions of costs and benefits that have little evidence supporting them. For this reason, the workshop concluded that there is an urgent need to undertake longitudinal studies of SDIs, paying particular attention to sub-national and regional SDIs and to application-driven approaches in which it is possible to identify stakeholders, user communities, and potential benefits (see Craglia and Nowak 2006[3]). As a follow-up to that workshop, the JRC commissioned the Centre of Land Policy and Valuations of the Universitat Politècnica de Catalonia to perform a study of the socioeconomic impact of SDI in Catalonia. The one-year study, which was concluded in December 2007, found that if the cost of topographic data production is excluded, the initial investment of €1.5 million over the period 2002-2006 was recovered in less than one year. The main categories of cost relate to the creation of metadata; setting up Internet services for discovery, view, and download; and preparation of the data for publication. Almost 80 percent of the costs were for human resources. The main benefits took the form of increased internal efficiency for public administrations (time saved in internal queries by technical staff, time saved in attending queries made by the public, and time saved in internal processes), effectiveness benefits (time saved by the public and by companies in dealing with public administration), and wider social benefits. One such social benefit was a narrowing of the digital divide for populations living in small communities, as in many cases these populations began to receive the same level of service that they would have received if they were living in larger towns and cities. Examples of such improved service included being able to contact governmental bodies at any time of the day or night and obtaining building permits faster.

The Catalonia study was important because for the first time it provided real evidence for both investment costs and measured benefits. It also allowed testing of the methodology proposed by the JRC, and it offered lessons learned for use in further studies. One such study is now in progress in the Regione Lombardia of Italy in collaboration with the JRC. It will be completed in 2009, paving the way for a wider deployment of the methodology across Europe. The full Catalonia study, which is also relevant for the wider assessment of PSI, is available at http://inspire.jrc.ec.europa.eu/reports/Study_reports/catalonia_impact_study_report.pdf.

---

[3] http://www.ec-gis.org/sdi//ws/costbenefit2006/reports/report_sdi_crossbenefit%20.pdf

12. Assessing the Economic and Social Benefits of NOAA Data Online[1]

Rodney Weiher
NOAA, United States

Let me start with a brief description of the mission and organization of the National Oceanic and Atmospheric Administration (NOAA) in order to better explain our role in PSI. NOAA's mission is two-fold. First, we seek to understand and predict changes in the Earth's environment, including weather, climate, oceans and the marine environment, and coastal resources. NOAA also manages the nation's offshore commercial fisheries and works with the states as a partner in managing coastal marine resources. In that sense, NOAA is a two-sided agency—scientific and regulatory.

There are five major operating units in NOAA. The National Weather Service, with which many people are familiar, issues basic forecast guidance in the United States and provides the observational infrastructure for atmospheric and weather information. It issues severe weather watches and warnings, which it is required to do by law, and it plays a major role in providing hydrological services, such as flood forecasts, to the country.

The National Environmental Satellite Data and Information Service (NESDIS) is the part of NOAA that operates the meteorological satellites, which feed into the National Weather Service's forecasts. NESDIS ensures that all of the atmospheric, climate, and ocean observation data is archived and available to the public.

The National Ocean Service is heavily involved in ocean and coastal mapping and charting as well as geodesy, and it provides services to the maritime industry, such as tides and current information. It also produces scientific and social science information for use in coastal management in partnership with states and local agencies.

The National Marine Fishery Service manages the commercial fisheries of the United States, including legislatively protected marine species, and collects scientific and social science data used in analysis aimed at improving management decisions in that area.

Finally, there is a strong research component to NOAA with the Office of Ocean and Atmospheric Research, and it is this office that provides much of applied research to NOAA in support of the mission goals outlined above.

NOAA is a major producer and user of digital networks. Observational data is intrinsic to the agency's mission, and it plays a major role in virtually every one of its activities, from foundational research to operational forecasts and warnings and regulatory decisions. NOAA operates more than ninety operational and research observing systems, which are associated with more than one hundred real-time and near-real-time information systems. These systems and the forecasts derived from them inform decisions that are important in various areas throughout the economy, and they include satellite, in-situ, buoy, ship, and aircraft observations; weather forecasts; tide and ocean

---

[1] Based on a presentation found at http://www.oecd.org/dataoecd/12/31/40066192.pdf

currents information; climate predictions; spatial temporal references such as nautical charts, GPS augmentations, and marine populations; and other scientific and social science information. So NOAA is in the information business and is arguably the biggest user and producer of operational scientific data in the federal government.

Regarding its policy towards the access and reuse of PSI, NOAA follows OMB Circular A-130, which is the guidance for the executive branch agencies in the federal government. As Nancy Weiss has described, Circular A-130 states that the open, efficient, and free exchange of federal government information is essential. Consequently, NOAA sets user fees at a level sufficient to recover the cost of dissemination but no higher, and, in particular, it does not charge prices to recover the capital costs. Thus, although there are some exceptions in such areas as national security, open access to data is the agency's policy.

What is the economic rationale for this policy? Kirsti Nilsen has already reviewed the professional literature. Basically, the underlying idea is that the information that NOAA generates has strong public good characteristics. First, it is difficult to exclude users, which makes it difficult to charge for the data in order to recoup the cost of the capital. Also, the marginal cost of producing additional information is essentially zero, so to charge for it would be non-optimal because it would exclude many users who value the data.

While NOAA provides the capital infrastructure—satellites, observing stations, distribution systems, and the like—the agency's policy calls generally for private industry to add value by generating and providing forecasts and other information for their customers, as appropriate. There is a whole body of literature that attempts to define "as appropriate," but the bottom line is that NOAA operates the infrastructure, and the private sector does the value-added part of it.

Of course, while public goods theory provides a rationale for publicly supplied information, it does not say how much publicly supplied information should be produced. So, consequently, NOAA has to make cost-benefit calculations in order to decide how much to produce. NOAA managers compare the net benefits of a particular system or data collection activity with other data systems and, ultimately, with other public investments, such as health or highways. The emphasis is on net benefits—the total lifetime system benefits less cost—rather than simple cost-benefit ratios, which can often be misleading as a guide to public investments. Cost-benefit analysis is essentially a social accounting structure, and it gives us an indication of whether the costs of a project are justified in terms of its benefits to society.

Moreover, recent advances in technology and the economics of observing systems make it necessary to carry out a case-by-case examination of whether the public goods argument is in fact still valid and justifies government funding. For instance, with the advent of the Internet and other technological advances, the costs of disseminating observations have come down dramatically, so, with the exception of the big satellites, it makes sense to reexamine the public goods argument for many of the new observing systems.

On the question of how to measure the benefits of NOAA's data, or even PSI in general, it is important to note that raw data, in and of themselves, do not provide value.

The data are input to a process that produces information that itself does have economic value. The benefits are thus derived from the resulting final product, and the value of the data is an imbedded good in that final product. An economist, thinking of the data from the point of view of a production function, will measure the marginal value of the data input in terms of the improvement it makes in the final output—say a forecast—and the value of that improvement to the forecast.

NOAA's products and services are used in both the public and the private sector. Much of the data goes directly to the private sector, where they lead both to productivity gains and to the creation of new products, services, and other business lines. It has led, for example, to better weather forecasts and advances in GPS, which in turn have led to efficiency gains and spawned a number of value-added industries in the United States. Furthermore, much of the data that NOAA collects is deemed essential for meeting NOAA's mission and legislative mandates, such as the protection of life and property. Thus NOAA data both help the agency meet important public mandates and also improve economic performance in the private sector, supporting applications in such areas as maritime commerce, energy, and transportation. In this way, PSI products affect economic decisions, and the way in which these decisions improve economic outcomes offers a measure of the value of the information.

According to the value of information theory in economics, information products and services have value if they affect decisions and change consequences. The value of that information is the increase in the expected benefits or the reduction in cost resulting from the information being available and being used versus not being available. For the information to have value, it must be used, and the value is determined by how much it improves decisions versus the situation where the information was not available.

There are several ways that the value of information theory has been used to value NOAA products and services. The first has been in modeling decisions made with and without the information and then asking what the expected consequences of those decisions are. One of the ways this approach has been used has been to estimate the benefits of seasonal data and forecasts in the agriculture sector. For example, a model can be made of how a farm would operate with the data that are presently available versus operations with an improved set of data. A second approach is to use self-assessment surveys to estimate what people would be willing to pay for information, which can lead to estimates of what economists call "consumer surplus," a measure of the benefits to society. A third approach is to use data from an "experiment"—looking at actual events and trying to estimate what the prior and the subsequent values of having the information were in that particular event. This was done, for example, in estimating the value of installing the NEXRAD system, the next-generation weather radars that the United States developed in the late 1980s and early 1990s. Weather-related fatalities and injuries were examined for the periods before and after NEXRAD was introduced, and a difference was found: a reduction in fatalities and injuries of about 40 percent.

In another case, NOAA had a major initiative to develop coastal and ocean observing systems, and a study[2] was done in 1977 to estimate the economic benefits of

---

[2] National Research Council. *The Ocean Observing System - Users, Benfits, and Priorities, Committee on the Global Ocean Observing System.* Ocean Studies Board. Commission on Geosciences, Environment,

these information systems. The benefits were estimated at more than $700 million annually, based on calculations of the value of information for a group of coastal and ocean-related industries—oil and gas, fishing, recreation, tourism, and two or three other large sectors.

There was also a series of studies done at NOAA on the benefits of real-time oceanographic data, i.e., tides and currents for different ports in the United States. In the Houston-Galveston Bay port—a large port in the Gulf of Mexico, used mainly for oil and gas imports—the benefits of such data are about $15 million a year annually. Compared to a $700 million benefit that is not a lot, but this is a much smaller system serving one location. If the benefits are added up across all the ports in the United States, a fairly good-sized number emerges.

As a final example of the value of NOAA data and information, consider an estimate of the value of daily weather forecasts in the United States. These benefits are called non-market use benefits; they do not have a market per se because forecasts are freely available on TVs, radio, newspapers, and the Internet. Thus the benefits cannot be measured by multiplying prices times the quantities sold because the goods are not exchanged in a market. Instead, by using state-of-the-art survey techniques and econometrics, it was estimated that there is a willingness to pay of about $103.64 per household for the approximately 110 million households in the United States, which leads to an estimated total of $11.4 billion in annual value (including $3 billion in a typical hurricane season alone). Because of this large value, the NOAA real-time weather data supplies a rapidly growing private weather service industry with sales, at last estimate, of well over $700 million annually, but this number is probably much larger now. In the United States and Europe, there is a growing weather derivatives financial industry, due primarily to the fact that the risk models have gotten so much better, and the industry uses the publicly supplied data to settle those derivatives. Essentially, utilities are hedging their bets on what the temperatures will be over the next three months in order to improve fuel buying and other decisions.

In summary, NOAA is a major producer and user of PSI in the United States, and NOAA's data is used throughout the economy. NOAA practices an open and free exchange of data and uses economic analysis, including calculating the benefits and costs of new and improved data in observing systems, to decide on the agency's investments and also to determine the appropriate public and private roles.

---

and Resources. National Academy Press, Washington, D.C. 1997.
http://fermat.nap.edu/openbook.php?isbn=0309056950

13. Exploring the Impacts of Enhanced Access to Publicly Funded Research[1]

John Houghton
Victoria University, Australia

In late 2006 Colin Steele, Peter Sheehan, and I produced a report for the Australian Department of Education, Science and Training (DEST) on the costs of research communication, emerging opportunities, and benefits.[2] The aims of the project were to explore and, where possible, to quantify the costs associated with research communication, focusing mainly on scientific publishing but also, to a lesser extent, on scientific data. The study also explored the potential benefits of enhanced access to research findings and tried to compare the costs and benefits of alternative access systems. The project was funded by the Australian government as a part of the government's consideration of open access policy and legislation, but it was also aimed at the funding agencies, research councils, and universities as a way of both providing input to their deliberations about access policies and offering a guide to the budgetary implications of alternative access models.

To explore the costs of interest, we developed an activity cost model that was based on an extensive review of the literature on the activities of research and the production of research findings. We adopted a systems perspective that was based on previous research by Donald King and colleagues in the United States.[3] The cost model included all the activities related to research, publishing and dissemination in higher education, and it covered databases as well as journals and books. Due to a lack of comparable data, all other private and public sector research activities were excluded.

Most of the costs associated with research communication are related to time—the time involved in reading, research, writing, peer review, and other tasks. To convert time to dollars, we used a model for full cost recovery that included salaries and overhead costs common in universities. In fact, it was based on the model for full cost recovery for non-laboratory-based contract research that is imposed on universities in Australia by the national competition policy.

One crucial aspect is the level at which costing is done. Research communication is multidimensional, so it is useful to take a matrix approach to costing that identifies the activities, actors, objects, functions, and, to a lesser extent, the applications with the aim of being able to break down the value chain and reassemble it along any of these dimensions. For example, activity costs can be reassembled as the cost of objects, such as the cost of producing a journal article; the cost for actors, such as the costs experienced

---

[1] Based on a presentation available at http://www.oecd.org/dataoecd/11/20/40067323.pdf
[2] Houghton, J. W., C. Steele, and P. J. Sheehan. 2006. *Research Communication Costs in Australia: Emerging Opportunities and Benefits.* Canberra: Department of Education, Science and Training. Found at http://dspace.anu.edu.au/handle/1885/44485
[3] See, for example, Tenopir, C. and D.W. King. 2000. *Towards Electronic Journals: Realities for Scientists, Librarians and Publishers.* Washington, DC: Special Libraries Association.

by universities or publishers in producing the article; and the cost of various functions, such as peer review of the article, quality control, and certification.

Costing the various activities involved in research communication, we found that reading is a major activity and that in Australian universities during 2005 the time spent on reading alone may have cost approximately A$5.8 billion. Reading by those researchers who were actively publishing in 2005 (i.e., reading in order to write) cost around A$3 billion. We estimated that writing scholarly, independent, peer-reviewed publications cost approximately A$640 million during 2005, and peer review and the editorial activities of academics cost approximately A$170 million. In sum, the estimated system-wide costs of the activities associated with core scholarly communication activities in Australian higher education came to approximately A$4 billion, or 30 percent of the total expenditure for higher education.

Having adopted a matrix approach,[4] we could then examine the activity costs in various ways. For example, summing the costs for objects suggested that, in 2005, producing a journal article in an Australian university cost, on average, A$21,000, excluding the research and reading time involved. By summing the costs for all actors, we calculated that writing all those journal articles counted in the Higher Education Research Data Collection cost the Australian National University approximately A$50 million in 2005.

In the second part of the study, we explored the potential benefits of enhanced access to research findings. Again, the analysis was based on an extensive review of the literature. It has been suggested that the most immediate benefits of enhanced access are probably felt within research itself, and these potential benefits might include increased speed of access resulting in a speeding up of the research and discovery process, a decrease in the amount of redundant research and a reduction in the investigation of blind alleys, and an increase in the efficiency of research and development. Wider access would also enable greater participation from poorer institutions and developing countries, provide more opportunities for interdisciplinary research and inter-sectoral collaboration, and allow researchers to study their fields more broadly, which could potentially lead to increased opportunities for commercialization.

---

[4] The following list of the various costs included in this actor/object matrix analysis may be helpful:
- Reading: academic staff ≈$5.8 billion, published staff ≈$3 billion pa.
- Writing (HERDC publications only)≈$636 million pa.
- Peer review(scaled to HERDC)≈$132 million pa.
- Editorial activities (scaled to published staff)≈$36 million pa.
- Editorial board activities (scaled to published staff)≈$3.8 million pa.
- Preparing grant applications(ARC & NHMRC)≈$110 million pa.
- Reviewing grant applications(ARC & NHMRC)≈$26 million pa.
- Publisher costs(scaled to HERDC)≈$164 million pa.
- Library acquisition costs (CAUL)≈$199 million pa.
- Library non-acquisition costs (CAUL)≈$321 million pa.
- Cost per download (sample of CAUL subscriptions)$3.51 (mean).
- ICT infrastructure(estimated total expenditure)≈$1billion pa.
- Sum of core activities ≈$4 billion (≈30% of HE expenditure).

Providing doctors, nurses, teachers, students, and small firms with a wider access to research findings may also lead to improvements in the quality of service and productivity in those areas of the economy, and it is also possible that the emergence of new industries could be encouraged by the availability of open-access content (e.g., weather derivatives based on access to meteorological data). For the wider community, potential benefits include such things as encouraging the development of informed citizens and informed consumers, who will be better able to make good decisions about the use of services like health and education and who will make better consumption choices. Ultimately, having informed citizens and informed consumers should increase the overall economic welfare of the country.

With such a wide range of potential benefits, the task of quantifying the impact of enhanced access is enormous, and there is no single definitive approach to the problem. Ideally, all the possible costs and benefits of all the possible alternative models for access would be accounted for, but that was beyond the scope of the project and may well be practically impossible.

In order to gain a preliminary sense of the overall effect of enhanced access, we chose to take a two-pronged approach. First, we explored some impact scenarios and case studies and then hypothesized about the possible effects of these scenarios on returns on R&D. Second, we modified a simple Solow-Swan[5] model and used it for our calculations.

There is a vast literature in economics that focuses on estimating the rate of return on R&D, and the returns quoted in that literature vary from time to time, place to place, and between fields of research. Nevertheless, we found certain patterns from that literature spanning a period of 20 to 25 years: Generally speaking, it is a characteristic finding that the rate of return is high, and it is typically in the range of 30 to 60 percent a year, sometimes higher.

The standard, neoclassical approach to estimating the rate of return on R&D makes some key simplifying assumptions:

- It assumes that all R&D generates knowledge that is useful in economic or social terms (i.e., the efficiency of R&D);

- It assumes that all knowledge is equally accessible to all entities that could make productive use of it (i.e., the accessibility of knowledge); and

- It assumes that all types of knowledge are equally substitutable across uses (i.e., the substitutability of knowledge).

The substitutability assumption is clearly not realistic, however, as a great deal of research is application specific, and much work has been done to address that fact. Much less work has been done to address the other two, equally unrealistic assumptions, and this is where we focused our efforts. Basically, we introduced accessibility and efficiency

---

[5] Solow, Robert. *A Contribution to the Theory of Economic Growth.* Quarterly Journal of Economics. Febuary 1956; Swan, Trevor. 2002. *Economic Growth.* The Economic Record. vol. 78. issue 243. pages 375-80.

into the standard model as negative or friction variables, and we then looked at the effect on returns to R&D of reducing the friction by increasing accessibility and efficiency.

There are a number of assumptions and caveats here. First, we assumed that the increase in accessibility and efficiency would be the same. Second, we assumed that a move to open access would have no net effect on the rates of accumulation or obsolescence of the stock of knowledge—the key word here being net. Third, we assumed that the information to which access was provided would indeed be discoverable.

We explored rates of return on R&D in the range of 25 to 75 percent, and we looked at increases in accessibility and efficiency in the range of 1 to 10 percent. For each category of R&D expenditure, we produced a table. Based on the review of the literature, we assumed a very conservative 25 percent social return on public sector R&D, and we suggested that a 5 percent increase in accessibility and efficiency would be plausible. Rates of return vary considerably, and the further one gets from the aggregate, the larger the range of uncertainty becomes. Nevertheless, to give an example:

- With government R&D funding in Australia at about A$6.5 billion in 2005 and a 25 percent return on R&D, a 5 percent increase in accessibility and efficiency would be worth around A$166 million a year;

- With higher education R&D at around A$4.3 billion, a 5 percent increase in accessibility and efficiency would be worth around A$110 million a year; and

- With the Research Council's competitive grants funding to higher education at around A$830 million, a 5 percent increase would be worth around A$20 million a year.

These are recurring annual gains from one year's R&D expenditure. Thus, if the change to enhanced access is a permanent one, they may be converted to growth rate effects.

It is possible to express some of these costs and impacts as benefit-cost ratios. For example, focusing on a limited range of costs, it is possible to compare the estimated incremental cost of open-access institutional repositories in higher education with the potential incremental benefits from enhanced access to higher education research, assuming that everything else remains the same. Again, there are a number of assumptions about the rates of increase of R&D expenditure, discount rates, risk premiums, and so on. Nevertheless, we estimated that over 20 years a national system of institutional repositories costing A$10 million a year would cost around A$130 million in net present value, whereas enhanced access to higher education research would be worth around A$4.8 billion in increased returns to R&D (in net present value); the resulting benefit-cost ratio would be 37. Similarly, enhanced access to the Research Council's competitive grants funding of higher education research, with benefits of around A$925 million, resulted in a calculated benefit-cost ratio of just over 7.

So what was learned from the study? Clearly, this is just one way to estimate the potential overall impacts of enhanced access to publicly funded research findings, and it has limitations and weaknesses. Perhaps its strength is its simplicity, bypassing the complexity of calculating the impact of each possible change. Ideally, it would be supplemented by detailed studies of how the impacts work in particular areas, that is, by more work on actual scenarios and developing those scenarios into detailed studies that would support the macroeconomic estimates.

The main critique of this sort of traditional approach from the point of view of new growth and evolutionary economics is that it does not take account all of the ways in which research makes contributions. Consequently, the impact estimates from this study may be viewed as being on the conservative side, which was the intention.

It is debatable whether this approach could be adopted to calculations outside R&D, as it depends on having estimates of returns to R&D spending. However, differences between scientific data and public sector information, such as meteorological or geological observation, are often quite small. They are simply another form of scientific observation. Consequently, it may be possible to apply the rates of return applicable to observational sciences to various forms of public sector information and to produce preliminary estimates of returns to public sector information.

DISCUSSION BY WORKSHOP PARTICIPANTS

PARTICIPANT: I would like to follow up. I do not think we should leave the impression that the U.S. federal government is monolithic in its policy and that everything is free and rosy. What I mean is that OMB Circular A-130 actually puts an upper bound for pricing at the incremental[1] cost of the information management system. So it actually can exceed the marginal[2] cost and often does. There is a lot of data and information sold at much more than the marginal cost of fulfilling the user request or the dissemination.

So not everything is free online, and there is quite a bit of information that is sold. Even at NOAA, the National Climatic Data Center, for example, which has all the retrospective archived climate data, charges fairly high fees for accessing those data. In fact, it funds about 30 percent of its annual operations through those sales, although I think the money actually goes to the treasury.

Until recently, Landsat images were $500 each, which was quite expensive. Even though it was substantially less than the French SPOT image, it was still a lot for an individual scene. So there is a large variance in the pricing of PSI in the federal government, even if the information is in the public domain.

I also should point out there is one exception to the public domain exclusion for federal government information from the Copyright Act, and that is in the National Institute of Standards and Technology. The Standard Reference Data Center has a legislative exemption from the exclusion and can copyright its standard reference data publications, and that may be the only exception to that in the federal government. I suppose that if someone were to not honor the copyright, they would not be sued by NIST, but nonetheless it does have a copyright in those publications.

So I just wanted to clarify that it is a very big system, and all the agencies really operate individually. There is an overall policy, and I think marginal cost pricing is the preferred option, but it can go up to incremental costs.

PARTICIPANT: I have one question, or actually a thought, after hearing these presentations. I was quite attracted to this methodology that I, in my mind, called deprivation method, in which you go to people and ask them, If we take oxygen away from you, how much would you pay to get it back? We hear this being applied to public sector information. I was just wondering, before I heard the last presentation by John Houghton, that since we are counting on information products or services that we already have, if we were to take those away, how much would we pay for getting them back? However, for the externalities and the innovation component, can you really go to end users and ask them how much they would pay for products which they do not have yet?

---

[1] In incremental cost pricing, "The price to secondary users is set so that revenues cover the cost to provide this incremental use, including recompiling the data, perhaps maintaining a computer site for downloading, purchasing CD-ROM blanks, recording the data, shipping to the user, and customer support, but not including the costs for the core service." National Research Council. 1997. *Bits of Power: Issues in Global Access to Scientific Data*, National Academy Press, pp. 125-126.

[2] In marginal cost pricing, "The cost to secondary users is set at the marginal cost of a specific unit sent to the user, including the cost of the CD-ROM blanks and postage and shipping. This price is lower than the incremental cost price, as long as the cost of output per unit declines when volume increases." Id. at p. 126.

PARTICIPANT: One thing I noticed in the literature is the assumption that one of the things that is asked is: How much?" "What is your time worth?" Most people will say that they are willing to spend a great deal more for information than they would, in fact, spend. Once you ask them to actually spend it, then their backs go up. They will say one thing, but they do not follow through if the price is, in fact, what they would say it should be. So you cannot really rely on their willingness to pay. The other alternative, then, is to say, "How much time are you saving?" which is considered to be more effective than asking what they are willing to pay.

PARTICIPANT: I would just add that if you are a public agency like NOAA that typically does not charge, the big problem is that it does not really know who the users are and what the user needs are. If you do not know who the users are and how they use the data, you do not know much about the marginal benefits. So I think one of the advantages of having free and open access is that there is no way that an economist can tell an agency what the market is going to be for something. Just making the data as widely available as you can, I think, is the way to maximize the benefits rather than sitting there trying to say, "What would someone be willing to pay for this product?" when the agency really does not have a good sense of how people use it. I totally agree that when you go out and ask people what they would be willing to pay, you will get numbers that are probably very inflated.

A final comment from a professional point of view: I do not think the data withdrawal approach is a good one because I just think that there are ex post facto questions, and there are huge substitution possibilities among sources of data. I think it is much better to try to estimate what the marginal benefit is of additional data or new data, if you can get some handle on that.

PARTICIPANT: Yes, on the NOAA data, you were focusing primarily on the economic kinds of uses, but I understand that a lot of the NOAA data are used in classrooms, that there is significant educational reuse of data that translates into not just the actual use but also the training of new scientists and that kind of thing. The other one being basic research—the use of the data for climate research and analysis, which obviously also has major benefits.

PARTICIPANT: Yes, I should have made it clear that I was mainly talking about operational data, but you are absolutely right about the research value of the data.

I was fascinated by John Houghton's presentation because of what we have been grappling with at NOAA. You think you have a big problem when you are trying to determine what the value of a better weather forecast is. The big problem we have is the value of the R&D, the research that NOAA is doing, and the last presentation gave me a few ideas about how to pursue this. There are a lot of uses for the data besides just the operational.

PARTICIPANT: Well, I have heard many interesting comments today. What has been lacking in general are some more views from industry about how they see the whole thing. I think it is a bit absent today. This is important when listening to the presentation of Robbin te Velde, who gave the impression that Dutch public sector bodies were left on their own to do whatever they thought was good for them. They were not told by the government what should be done. They could charge or not, depending on their own wishes. We are told that there will be some resistance for change, so it seems that this is only a supply issue.

I would be really interested to hear much more about companies and what are they doing to fight when systems do not work well, because one of the things that is lacking, at least in Europe, is solid complaints. The European Court of Justice has not received a single case related to public sector information. I think that it is important to look at the judicial perspective.

I also was very much interested by the comment of our Google colleague, who reported today about their work with the U.S. government to see how they can work together in order to get good information for reuse.

That brings me to the NOAA. Sometimes it seems to me that you are working in a very competitive model with private companies, but not competing directly with them. They are your users. You work together. You build a better world together.

I would be interested to know whether the private companies in the EU would tell me that this is the way they look to the work with European Met offices and whether this is the view that European Met offices have about work with the users. The question is, what works better—i.e., how can we work together, private and public, not working against public sector policy, but working together with public sector policy?

PARTICIPANT: Recalling what Dr. Fornefeld presented this morning about the value change of the PSI data and about how data has to be combined together so that services can be provided, I think we come back to this once again because the economic models that Ms. Nilsen presented say that the product has to be sold for the marginal costs. That is right, but it does not take into account the investments that are needed. When you sell a product at the marginal cost, you do not take into account the investment required to produce these goods.

In the case of information, the marginal cost is nearly zero because it is very easy to distribute information over the Internet. So we can state that the bulk of the cost of information, from our discussion today, is investment cost. That is why you cannot sell information, because if you want to price information in its marginal cost, it makes no economic sense to sell information.

But, as you remember from this morning, to provide services based on this information does have marginal cost. There is also a business opportunity to sell your services along with the information. It makes no sense for anybody to sell information priced at marginal cost because it has no marginal cost, but it does make sense to sell services.

In the public sector debate, we speak about public sector information holders who sell information to reusers under certain licensing terms, and this is considered all right because we see it as acceptable to sell information to the people who are going to provide services. When we look at this value chain, we say information should not be sold, but the service should be sold. However, we must remember that there is no such thing as a free lunch. The information producer should realize some return of the profits as well. The producer needs to cover the investment costs of producing the information. I have very seldom seen a business model based on the notion that the information will be provided free to a service provider, but a certain percentage of the profit of the service provider will come back to the data producer. This would be an integration into a new value chain. There would be an agreement of cooperation between the data producer and the service provider, and the data would not be permitted to be sold by the service provider. The only thing that is sold is the service, but a part of the profit derived from selling the service would come back to the data producer.

The licensing could be easier because it is an agreement between the data producer and the service provider. That is not how it is today—the price of the information and the licensing depends on the business model of the service provider.

For example, perhaps a local government could provide cartographic information to a small company that wants to provide services based on this cartographical information. The small company has to explain its business model to the local government, so that the local government could set the price. They might ask how many users do you intend to have, or at what rate would you want to price your service, and then the local government would set a price. This is very difficult for innovating companies because they do not know their market. They do not know the price or the benefits they have to make of it, and they have to first pay for the information before they can go into business. This way no innovation can work, and it is really an inhibition to innovation by small companies that are not able to prepay for the information.

PARTICIPANT: My company has a very positive working relationship with many different public agencies when it comes to the sharing and dissemination of data. That is not really something that is controversial or problematic. But industry is interested, as more technology and services develop, in being able to provide complex datasets not only to other companies or other customers but also to users in order to unleash the kind of creativity leading to new applications or innovations. So what industry would like to ensure—at least what my company is looking for—is that the usually positive initial contact between government and industry continues to be positive. In a previous life I worked for an industry association that handled PSI questions, and I saw there at least two examples of very negative cases that will probably end up in court when the PSI Directive has been implemented in Sweden, and we will see if they end up in the European Court of Justice. It is clearly a risk that this initially very positive contact becomes harsher or more problematic when the depth of access requested by private companies and industries increases. I hope, of course, that this will not be the case. I think that there is most definitely a demand side in private industry to complement the supply side in the government as in the discussion we are having here today.

PARTICIPANT: I know others are quite rightly saying, "Where are the complaints? Where are the cases that people bring?" I think what we all have to acknowledge is that it is extraordinarily difficult for the private sector to take on the public sector in a court of law. It is a big step, especially if you are a small company. I think also there is the question of time, or timeliness. If a company has an idea that it wants to develop but in order to develop it, it has to go to court, then the idea is dead before it emerges into the real world.

I have a special relationship with one particular trading fund, and that has caused us, as a business, more grief than I would have thought possible. I think one of the reasons for that is that public sector bodies, understandably, do not like being attacked. If you were to attack a supermarket, for example, on fair and reasonable grounds, if it is a well-run business you are likely to get a sensible, moderate response. That is not necessary true of state-run organizations that do not feel that they are able to defend themselves in the same way. So in dealing with a state-run organization, you have to really believe that the relationship has gone to a point of no return before you take action.

There are two other points I would like to make. The first is that obviously you have to go through the national process before you can then get to the broader EU level. That can be quite telling. Once you get as far as the EU, then I think the situation becomes a great deal more interesting. The EU institutions have got a different slant on some of these issues.

Secondly, I think the competition authorities in various EU countries may have a great deal of ability to unlock some of these problems for all of us. It only takes one or two decisions and all of a sudden the whole of Europe will have to take an interest in this issue.

PART THREE

14. Measuring the Social and Economic Costs and Benefits of Public Sector Information Online: A Review of the Literature and Future Directions

Paul F. Uhlir, Raed M. Sharif, and Tilman Merz

The second day of the workshop was devoted to a discussion of the issues by all of the participants, first in two breakout sessions and then in a combined, plenary format. The two breakout sessions were preceded by a presentation entitled Measuring the Social and Economic Costs and Benefits of Public Sector Information (PSI) Online: A Review of the Literature and Future Directions, which was prepared by Paul F. Uhlir, Raed M. Sharif, and Tilman Merz.[1] The topics covered by this presentation included: (1) the benefits of access to and reuse of PSI; (2) government policies; (3) a review of the literature about measuring the PSI reuse market and linking outcomes to access regimes; (4) a critique and challenges of current measurement approaches; (5) suggestions for future directions; and (6) questions for further discussion.

First, access to and reuse of PSI in the online environment has direct and indirect economic and social benefits. By developing new markets online, the information industries help enhance the efficiencies of other industries, and, consequently, individuals are empowered as economic actors. Moreover, performance within the public sector is improved, and innovative research projects are fostered. Making PSI available online benefits society through improved political transparency, enhanced educational and research opportunities, and the support of personal decision-making capabilities.

Second, different governments vary markedly in their policies and approaches to dealing with PSI online. In the United States, access to government information is established by a number of laws, including the 1995 Paperwork Reduction Act, the Sunshine in Government Act, and the Freedom of Information Act. (See the summary of the presentation by Nancy Weiss.) In the European Union, many countries and government institutions use a cost recovery model and limit the reuse of PSI by applying intellectual property protections. At the same time, there is an emphasis on producing higher-quality and less restricted information, following the 2003 PSI Directive. There are also various hybrid models adopted in the EU and other countries.

In determining PSI policy, the best approach is clear: (1) equal treatment and competition; (2) minimizing the transaction costs necessary to obtain PSI; (3) transparency of access conditions and data characteristics through the availability of good metadata; and (4) accountability. Beyond that, PSI policy is governed by a variety of complex interrelations that reflect the scope of public sector activity in information provision, information quality, access and discoverability, and pricing. Which policy is best under these various conditions is less clear and may be context-dependent.

---

[1] Found at http://www.oecd.org/dataoecd/23/42/40170933.ppt

Third, in analyzing open access and cost recovery policies, there have already been a number of studies that have resulted in assessments and empirical measurements. The resulting literature review, which is not comprehensive, is summarized in Table 1.

TABLE 1 Assessments of PSI Activities in Chronological Order, 2008-1998

Study Title	Author(s) and year
Models of Public Sector Information Provision via Trading Funds[2]	David Newbery, Lionel Bently, and Rufus Pollock. 2008.
EcoGeo Project[3]	Stéphane Roche, et al. 2007.
Fair Use in the U.S. Economy: Economic Contribution of Industries Relying on Fair Use[4]	Thomas Rogers and Andrew Szamosszegi. 2007.
The Power of Information: An Independent Review[5]	Ed Mayo and Tom Steinberg. 2007.
The Socio-Economic Impact of the Spatial Data Infrastructure of Catalonia[6]	Pilar Garcia Almirall, Montse Moix Bergadà, and Pau Queraltó Ros. Edited by Max Craglia. 2007; published 2008.
Benefits of the New GPS Civil Signal: The L2C Study[7]	Irving Leveson. 2006.
The Commercial Use of Public Information (CUPI)[8]	Office of Fair Trading, United Kingdom. 2006.
Developing Geographic Information Infrastructures: The Role of Information Policies[9]	Bastiaan Van Loenen. 2006.
Economic Impact of Open Source Software on Innovation and the	Rishab Aiyer Ghosh, et al. 2006.

---

[2] Found at http://www.opsi.gov.uk/advice/poi/models-psi-via-trading-funds.pdf
[3] Web site: http://ecogeo.scg.ulaval.ca
[4] Found at http://www.ccianet.org/artmanager/uploads/1/FairUseStudy-Sep12.pdf
[5] Found at http://www.cabinetoffice.gov.uk/media/cabinetoffice/strategy/assets/power_information.pdf
[6] Found at http://inspire.jrc.ec.europa.eu/reports/Study_reports/catalonia_impact_study_report.pdf
[7] Found at http://www.insidegnss.com/auto/0706%20Benefits.pdf
[8] Found at http://www.opsi.gov.uk/advice/poi/oft-cupi.pdf
[9] Found at http://repository.tudelft.nl/file/107024/088301

Study Title	Author(s) and year
Competitiveness of the Information and Communication Technologies (ICT) Sector in the EU[10]	
MEPSIR, Measuring European Public Sector Information Resources[11]	Makx Dekkers, Femke Polman, Robbin te Velde, and Marc de Vries. 2006.
Economic Value of the Nova Scotia Ocean Sector[12]	Michael Gardner, Robert Fraser, Mike Milloy, and James Frost. 2005.
Estimating Economic Benefits from NOAA PORTS® Information: A Case Study of Tampa Bay[13]	Hauke Kite-Powell. 2005.
Estimating the Economic Benefits of Regional Ocean Observing Systems[14]	Hauke Kite-Powell, Charles Colgan, et al. 2004.
The Value of Snow and Snow Information Services[15]	Richard Adams, Laurie Houston, and Rodney Weiher. 2004.
The Economic Benefit of the BGS (British Geological Survey)[16]	Roger Tym and Partners. 2003.
Borders in Cyberspace: Conflicting Public Sector Information Policies and Their Economic Impacts[17]	Peter Weiss. 2002.
Economic Framework for Meteorological Service Provision	Don Gunasekera. 2002.
Economic Value of Current and Improved Weather Forecasts in the U.S. Household Sector[18]	Jeffrey Lazo and Lauraine Chestnut. 2002.

---

[10] Found at http://ec.europa.eu/enterprise/ict/policy/doc/2006-11-20-flossimpact.pdf
[11] Found at http://www.epsiplus.net/reports/mepsir_measuring_european_public_sector_resources_report
[12] Found at http://www.mar.dfo-mpo.gc.ca/pande/ecn/ns/e/ns-e.pdf
[13] Found at http://tidesandcurrents.noaa.gov/publications/Estimated_Economic_Benefits_from_NOAA_PORTS_report.pdf.
[14] Found at http://www.nopp.org/nopp/project-reports/reports/04powell.pdf.
[15] Found at http://www.economics.noaa.gov/bibliography/econ-value-snow-final-report.doc
[16] Found at http://www.bgs.ac.uk/downloads/start.cfm?id=380
[17] Found at http://www.epsiplus.net/reports/borders_in_cyberspace
[18] Exec. summary: http://ftp.wmo.int/pages//prog/amp/pwsp/documents/JeffLazo_Household_Value_Study_ExecSumm.pdf

Study Title	Author(s) and year
Canadian Geospatial Data Policy Study[19]	Garry Sears. 2001.
Environmental Data (various studies)	U.S. National Academy of Sciences. 2001.
Prosperity Effects of Different Pricing Models for PSI	Dutch Ministry of the Interior. 2001.
Economic Effects of Open Access Policies for Spatial Data	Dutch Federal Geographic Data Committee. 2000.
Economic Framework for the Provision of Meteorological Services	John Zillman and John Freebairn. 2000.
Commercial Exploitation of Europe's Public Sector Information[20]	Pira International Ltd., University of East Anglia, and KnowledgeView Ltd. 2000.
The Economic Contribution of Ordnance Survey GB [Great Britain][21]	OXERA, Oxford Economic Research Associates Ltd. 1999.
The Dissemination of Spatial Data: A North American-European Comparative Study on the Impact of Government Information Policy	Xavier Lopez. 1998.

Table 2 provides an overview of the data collection and measurement techniques used in these studies.

---

[19] Executive summary: http://www.geoconnections.org/programsCommittees/proCom_policy/keyDocs/KPMG/KPMG_E.pdf
[20] Exec. summary: http://www.ekt.gr/cordis/news/eu/2001/01-01-19econtent/econtent_study2.pdf
[21] Found at http://www.ordnancesurvey.co.uk/oswebsite/aboutus/reports/oxera/oxera.pdf

TABLE 2 Data Collection and Measurement Techniques Used in Assessments of PSI Activities

Data Sources	Data Collection Methods	Techniques	Methodological Approaches
Primary sources: Industry, government, end users	Desk research	Estimate of overall PSI market size based on estimates of respondents	Market based approaches
	Web survey		
	Online questionnaires	Estimate of overall PSI market size based on turnover	Normative or prescriptive decision-making models
Secondary sources: Mainly government data (e.g., GDP, household income, employment, payroll, and exports) and industry reports	Interviews		
	Review of relevant documents, literature and international trends	Self-reporting	Descriptive behavioral response methods
		International comparisons	
	In-depth case studies		Contingent valuation method
		Social surplus approach (difference between the willingness to pay for PSI minus the cost of supplying it)	
	Focus groups		Conjoint analysis
	Delphi technique or expert opinion		Economy-wide analysis
		Application of Bayesian decision theory	
		Projection, scenario analysis, expert opinion, and team consensus approaches	
		General equilibrium model	

It should be noted that most of these studies did not explain in detail why a certain technique or approach was used. Collectively, the conclusion was that the economic and equity arguments concerning access to and reuse of PSI are complex and deserve considerably more analysis and policy attention. Thus specific estimates should be looked at with caution.

Fourth, in extending this critique to identify ongoing challenges in measuring PSI in the online environment, current methodological approaches have several weakness. The scope of these studies is limited, for example, and more country, regional, and global scale studies, as well as more comparative analyses at the country and regional levels, are needed. There are also few longitudinal studies, which are needed in order to make comparisons across countries or over time. Furthermore, the existing studies have often used top-down approaches to determine the values of PSI products, overestimating the true value of PSI to the economy by ignoring the substitutes available in the absence of PSI. In effect, this methodology can only demonstrate the "value that can be linked with PSI" rather than the value of PSI itself (Office of Fair Trading, United Kingdom, 2006 at http://www.oft.gov.uk/shared_oft/reports/consumer_protection/oft861.pdf).

Further academic and empirical research is needed to supply what is lacking in these existing studies—in particular, a multidisciplinary or multidimensional approach and a focus on individual reuse of PSI. Future studies should also work on improving reliability by addressing the lack of strong theoretical foundations and robust data collection. For example, the longstanding difficulty of securing the quality data needed to separate PSI-dependent sectors from the rest of the information economy (e.g., in national accounts and industrial or product classifications) remains a problem, complicated even more by the heterogeneity of PSI. Consequently, the economic value of PSI is hard to measure via shares of GDP, as substitutes for PSI-derived products lead to an overestimation of such contributions.

Fifth, in suggesting future directions, one worthy goal could be to develop a manual for data collection and analysis of PSI policies. This manual could involve statisticians (e.g., EUROSTAT), national accountants (e.g., from the government finance ministries), and other PSI experts. A similar model was used successfully in 1999 by OECD in cooperation with EUROSTAT to produce a manual on data collection and analysis in the environmental goods and services industry.

Other possible goals include creating a digital repository of PSI-related content and promoting and facilitating academic-focused research that is informed by well-established theories and methodologies. Involving young scholars and scientists in this process is essential. Such research also needs to pay special attention to more individual uses of PSI.

Finally, the authors proposed several questions as essential for ongoing discussion:

1. What are the commonalities and differences among the various analytical methods identified and presented?

2. What are the most effective metrics or indicators for the assessment of particular kinds of information and policies? What approaches and metrics or indicators can be used to effectively measure the network effects of the use of PSI online?

3. What are the main strengths and weaknesses of these approaches, including such factors as their accuracy, comprehensiveness, relevance, validity, and reliability?

4. What still needs to be learned about applying these methods to the evaluation of public information policies in the online environment?

5. What theoretical frameworks, models, and best practices used in assessing other information products or services can be applied to the assessment of the policies of access to and reuse of digital PSI?

6. What future directions might be pursued for the better study and measurement of access to and reuse of PSI online?

7. What other questions or issues should be raised in this context?

15. Summary of the First Breakout Session

Juan Carlos de Martin, Rapporteur

The discussion in this breakout session focused on three main questions:

1. What are the main strengths and weaknesses of the methodologies used so far?
2. Are there theoretical frameworks emerging that could be useful to assess the management of PSI?
3. What are some new directions that could be taken?

To begin with the main strengths and weaknesses of existing methodologies, it was noted that no methodology seems clearly superior, or general enough to be singled out as superior. More research and testing of various methodologies is needed. It may turn out that PSI is such a diverse field that there is no single assessment methodology that will be relevant to all PSI categories and contexts and that instead a variety of methodologies may be needed, depending on the type, size, and importance of PSI.

What are the theoretical frameworks? Fortunately, PSI does not start in a vacuum because there are a number of related subjects that could be drawn from, such as open-access models in scientific publishing. An interesting body of research and data already exists on this topic, as described in Professor Houghton's presentation as well as in various reports by experts and research funding agencies across the globe. This is a topic that is very similar to PSI and, indeed, could be viewed as a subset of PSI. In looking for theoretical frameworks to use with PSI, one can examine this and other related methodologies to see if there are useful lessons that can be learned and applied.

A related topic that emerged in the breakout session is open source and free software. This is a well-established subject area, and there are very interesting assessment reports, such as the one funded by the European Commission on the assessment of free software, from which one might draw some insights that can be used in the assessment of PSI effects.

Finally, some specific areas of PSI, such as meteorological data and geographic information, already have a body of assessment experience, and we can look at the way that those sectors have been assessed to see if the approaches can be generalized, at least to some extent, for other types of public sector information.

Several participants brought up the role of the public sector, which had already been touched upon earlier. What is the role of public sector, and what kind of information should the public sector produce or not produce? Should its role, for example, include value-added services? This may be too complex a question to hope for an answer that will apply equally to all countries.

Even if one considers just the countries in the European Union, many of them differ in their approaches to this subject. This variety of approaches may hold a richness that can be taken advantage of, with different best practices emerging in different countries. After a few years of studying this heterogeneous way of approaching these problems, we may be able to understand more about such fundamental questions.

The third question concerned the identification of practical actions that could be taken. The overview presentation that started the breakout session made three specific suggestions: an OECD public sector information manual, an online repository of assessment methods, and the identification of some areas of further academic research.

The idea for an OECD PSI manual was inspired by a 1999 OECD publication, *The Environmental Goods & Services Industry—Manual for Data Collection and Analysis*. Such a manual could be used to assess the implementation of the upcoming OECD PSI principles. One question that was raised in the discussion concerned the audience for this manual: Who is it for? There are the practitioners, of course, the experts such as those at this workshop, and even if only the practitioners were interested in the manual, the effort of creating it would probably be worthwhile nonetheless. Fortunately, the audience will probably be larger than that. The PSI producer and reuser community also could be interested, and the "accountants"—meaning whoever in the public sector will have to try to quantify the impact of PSI reuse—would be part of the audience as well.

Another question was: What should be the functions of a manual like that? There are at least three main functions. First, there should be an effort to clarify the extent and kinds of public sector information that are available. Of course, some of this information is already available in reports and research papers. Nevertheless, a shared, consensus taxonomy of public sector information would be worthwhile content to include in a manual like this. Second, it would be useful to have a collection of compatible assessment practices. The assessment practices in use today across Europe are widely different, and a manual like this could offer guidelines for performing certain evaluation processes in a more homogeneous way. The third function of a manual of this sort would be to involve more bodies than is the case today, including national or supranational statistical bodies.

Another point that participants in this breakout session discussed was: Who are the stakeholders for a manual like this, and how could the OECD involve them? During the course of the discussion a very preliminary list of potential stakeholders was compiled. These included not only the PSI holders and those organizations at the center of the discussion in this workshop but also non-governmental organizations or associations that need public sector information for their activities. Another group would be libraries interested in public sector information along with scientific, technical, and medical publishers. Other sectors and communities, such as the health, meteorological, and geographical information sectors, are important for at least two reasons. First, they already have considerable experience in evaluation methods, and, second, in some cases there is no unified approach to PSI, so focusing on the sectoral bodies is the only way to address such relevant communities.

The second main point of discussion on the third question concerned a possible PSI repository. "Repository" is now a fashionable concept because of the open-access movement and the development of many open institutional repositories. But why a repository? Exactly what kind of repository? That was the starting point for the discussion, but the idea of a repository quickly shifted to the concept of an online portal or platform. It was noted first that a repository suggests something rather passive. Of course, this does not necessarily imply something negative, as a repository contains information that is a crucial building block for other activities. The breakout group spent some time discussing the simple case of a passive repository and what kind of information might go into that. The information need not be limited to just research results concerning assessments of PSI, for example. A collection of best practices would be useful because they are relevant for governments; other relevant information might include users' case studies and principles. But perhaps the user community may want something less passive and more proactive—a platform that encourages the creation of content. This might include a wiki, a discussion forum, a mailing list, and so on.

A potential starting point described earlier in this workshop is the existing ePSI*plus* Web site and repository. Although it is a wonderful repository, it is, by design EU-specific. Furthermore, there is some question of the long-term existence of this repository because it is linked to a project with a three-year duration. Just as paper information can be preserved for centuries, any repository would need to be designed with information preservation ensured over the long term.

More generally, there is an issue of language that is important for some countries and less so for others but which needs to be considered if one is designing a platform with a global reach. There also is the question of involving specific established communities, such as the geographic information community, in a general purpose PSI portal.

Session participants emphasized the value of such a repository for developing countries. Such a repository could serve as a tool to help PSI managers and policy makers in less economically developed countries understand the value of PSI and learn about current practices in its management and use. Many experts on PSI in the developing world would appreciate having such an online resource.

The final major area of discussion concerned academic research. In the overview presentation at the beginning of the breakout session, there was a list of specific topics that academic research might address, including individual users of PSI and the social effects; network effects and network externalities, both positive and negative; the role of automated knowledge extraction and reuse; pilot projects to test different approaches; and promoting the involvement of young scientists.

In addition to this core list of potential topics, there is the question of how to encourage this type of research. If research funding agencies and foundations were to include PSI assessment within their research topics, this could be an effective way of encouraging research in this arena. Another approach would be to hold open workshops and conferences, bringing together people from different disciplines in the traditional academic way but focused on this new challenging topic. An online journal could also be useful. Since this is a relatively new, multidisciplinary topic, articles about it are spread across many different journals. One could do a feasibility study to see if there is a case for a specific PSI journal. And finally, awards or scholarships for theses and dissertations in this area could be a way to involve young scholars and scientists in this new and difficult research topic. Perhaps the manual itself could be undertaken as an academic initiative and involve young scholars and scientists in its planning and development.

16. Summary of the Second Breakout Session

Tilman Merz, Rapporteur

This group had a very creative and spirited discussion, but it was not exactly structured according to the questions given in the outline. To begin with, there was some discussion about questionnaires and how they could be designed to make sure that they are comparable. In the past, the OECD has issued model questionnaires, which could also be an option for the future.

A number of comments centered on the value chains of public sector information use and reuse. To understand where value is created and where the obstacles and costs lie, we need to have a clear understanding of the different value chains, and throughout the discussion, ideas for further studies came up.

After the OECD policy principles are issued at the OECD Ministerial Conference in June 2008, there will be reviews of the principles and whether they are being applied. The OECD also will address the issue of whether its members are addressing the right questions about PSI and access to PSI. These topics formed the broad subject matter of the discussion.

Some participants said that policy makers need hard facts for making informed decisions. They need to be able to compare data and methodologies across countries and possibly also focus research on top PSI sectors, but there is a difficulty in that the PSI sectors deemed most important may differ from country to country.

It was suggested that comparisons be made between country-sector combinations, perhaps starting with those sectors that are most often cited, such as meteorological and geospatial information. In doing so, different political and institutional contexts will have to be taken into account. The idea was raised of using different regions within the same country to conduct studies because quite often this will provide institutional contexts that are more similar. Even this may not always work, however. In Eastern Europe, for example, there are frequently differences in how PSI policy works between the capital and the more rural areas.

The OECD PSI principles that are forthcoming will seek to promote broad dissemination of PSI at the lowest cost possible. It will be important in the future to review not only the implementation of these principles but also the costs that public sector bodies may accrue from applying these principles and also any obstacles that arise when attempting to apply them.

Another area of discussion was how to define PSI products. Definitions are needed in order to better structure studies and also to compare studies. There also needs to be a consensus on exactly what PSI products are. Some discussants noted it might be better to take a functional approach than to take an approach based on defining PSI products. This is an area, therefore, where further research may be justified.

The breakout group discussed the online repository of PSI-related information at some length. Such a repository could contain surveys or questionnaires and their results (including those of the OECD), contacts for further research, best practices in PSI policy, licenses available for PSI in different countries, and even a listing of different types of PSI.

The repository would need to be well organized and structured. The ePSI*plus* Network collects a great deal of information on PSI, and it is already connected to many other studies. Thus the repository could build on this model. Many of the participants thought that it could be valuable to share more information and approaches to measuring impacts of PSI policy.

Another topic of discussion was data collection. One obstacle to data collection is that countries have different national accounting practices, which makes analysis of PSI market development very difficult. Some kind of international cooperation therefore might be needed in this area. While at a national level, PSI sectors and PSI products may be isolated, international industry and product classifications usually do not allow such separation and generally lump several different content or service industries together with PSI-based ones.

The difficulties of obtaining data on the use and reuse of PSI (or PSI market development more generally) were discussed as well. The academics and sometimes even the private-sector bodies that conduct surveys on PSI use generally do not have the authority to demand the submission of data. For example, the OFT indicated that it is sometimes in a better position to elicit responses from government bodies. Therefore, it may be useful to involve government competition bodies in this process, because in certain cases they may have better access to data.

The need for a theoretical model of expected benefits was highlighted as well. The e-government economic programs were mentioned as one potentially useful example. There may be some parallels between them and PSI use in terms of the theoretical model of expected benefits; PSI research may thus benefit from examining these models.

Another area of discussion was how best to learn about the issues that users and reusers of PSI are facing. Participants raised a number of ideas, including suggestions for data collection methods, such as how to get in touch with users and reusers and how to group respondents. One suggested approach is to announce new PSI research that is relevant for reusers so that reusing businesses could be identified. Publicly funded libraries can be used for disseminating PSI to citizens and for research on the users and reusers of such information. Publicly funded libraries are often used as a cost-effective way for disseminating government data, especially in North America and Scandinavia.

The mapping of the value chain of PSI came up a number of times. The suggestion was made that the value chain could be modeled in terms of activities or business processes, attaching costs to the value chain. The underlying idea is to make studies more comparable by linking them to value chains.

Participants also suggested a number of ideas for further studies on PSI, including the transition costs of switching PSI policy regimes (e.g., the cost-benefit analysis of moving away from the U.K. trading fund model that was introduced in the 1980s), the substitution of PSI by private-sector-generated data, examining licensing costs in different areas of PSI, and the extent of network externalities of online PSI.

Finally, participants thought it might be interesting to look at other subject areas in order to learn from comparable situations. For instance, one might examine value generation from free online access in terms of the parallels it has with the economic impacts of the liberalization of telecoms.

PART FOUR

17. General Discussion of Results from the Breakout Sessions and Possible Next Steps

Paul F. Uhlir, Rapporteur

The two sessions resulted in quite similar conclusions, although there were also a few differences. Some of the participants in Session A were not fully convinced that a repository of PSI research and methods is justified at this point, for instance, whereas those in Session B discussed what the contents of such a repository should be. The Session A group identified more funding sources for academic research than just the European Commission.

The participants in Session B highlighted the fact that PSI research has failed to map the value chain. This is an interesting point and is something that the OECD Working Party on Information Economy has examined in a number of areas in digital content.

One issue that came up less than might have been expected was the international dimension of PSI and related data collection. International harmonization or international cooperation are issue areas that academic research might be able to address.

When discussing research, one should not consider only academic research because there are other kinds of research commissioned by governments. There can be competitive studies that governments launch in this area, and governments are doing internal studies as well. For instance, general accounting offices or PSI offices could study the procedures and the organization of the administration of PSI.

Many governments are doing research on PSI, and governments are very important for academic research. The question is: Where should the funding for academic research studies come from, and who will commission them?

One of the great benefits of creating an open digital repository of PSI-related content would be its value for developing countries in which little or even no discussion, implementation, or experience exists in the area of PSI. Such a repository could become a credible resource for these countries to use, and it would provide them the opportunity to learn from the experiences of other countries, thus saving the time and effort needed to initiate such research from the beginning.

Another point about repositories is that it is important not to replicate what is already there. The European Commission and the ePSI*plus* project already have many resources online. A repository could link to those resources and fill in the gaps without replicating them.

The participants in Session A also discussed an online journal in connection with the repository. These two activities could be quite helpful and related. A repository is a place to make available materials such as questionnaires, results, or benchmarking of publicly funded PSI studies. It can be more difficult to include results of academic research, however, because research published in proprietary subscription journals may be prohibited from being deposited in publicly accessible repositories. Any repository is compromised if research that needs to be disseminated quickly and broadly cannot be disseminated openly.

It is not desirable to disseminate research linked to PSI in a journal that is expensive to readers or that takes a long time from when an article is submitted to the time it is published. These considerations were taken into account when the International Journal of Spatial Data Infrastructure Research was launched. It is an online journal published by the European Commission that is free and is available at http://ijsdir.jrc.ec.europa.eu.

It uses the Creative Commons licensing so that authors retain their full rights, and it is listed in the directory of open access journals, which adds to its visibility. As soon as an author submits an article, it is published on the web in a review session. This means that one's research is disseminated immediately, even before it goes through the peer-review process. Therefore, if an author is looking for an online academic outlet to disseminate research in this area, the International Journal of Spatial Data Infrastructure Research is a potential vehicle, and it is one way in which the European Commission is supporting this type of activity. An online PSI journal could emulate this model.

One issue requiring further clarification is that there were somewhat different ideas between breakout groups A and B about what an online repository is. Group B talked about repositories in the context of exchanging information about surveys and questionnaires. The subject came up in the context of surveying businesses. To that end, the Office of Fair Trade reported that it had very good success with surveying PSI holders and businesses who were using PSI information. However, the discussion focused more broadly on exchanging information about surveys, what the reasons are for doing this, and what the big questions are that one is trying to address. Only after reaching consensus on those issues would it make sense to try to work out ways to develop a common survey questionnaire or to add questions to existing surveys.

Group A considered this focus on surveys as just one function within an active repository platform. The discussion in that group noted that it is important to emphasize the main goal here: to maximize and optimize the economic and social values of PSI. The repository, the manual, and the research are means to supporting that end.

There are countries that are now applying policies that are not in good agreement with the PSI principles being developed by the OECD. Principles are fine, but they may be forgotten or ignored even before they are adopted. They will be useless if they are not taken one step further.

In order to maximize the economic and social values of any PSI repository, representatives of the member states or of the organizations involved will need to be consulted by repository managers on how to mobilize all stakeholder communities. The autonomy that these representatives have in deciding their agenda may be limited. Then the repository managers will need to contact businesses, which are crucial in changing mindsets and which may also be able to do part of the work. Success will not happen overnight, but these repositories are the places in which information may be put together and good practices shared.

Furthermore, a repository may be the best way to support the micro-entity, the individual, or the very small business. Must they go through a steep learning curve, or is it possible to find ways to help them move forward quickly? It is possible that many who have tried to reuse PSI for business or otherwise have found that it is not so easy and have become disenchanted. In such cases the opportunities are lost, so it is important to give reusers of PSI some help.

Enhancing the functionality of an online repository is another possible goal. The idea here would be to create an open knowledge environment in which one could take the OECD principles and organize an interactive discussion relating to each principle about how best to promote it, how to measure it, and what body of work exists that is relevant to it. It would then be possible to create a community around the discussion of those principles in order to diffuse and implement them, whether that discussion goes on among practitioners within the government, the various interest groups in the user community, academics, or others. Such ongoing discussions would help solve the problem of the principles being forgotten or ignored because in these discussions the principles become living recommendations or organizing principles around which the body of knowledge is created. Of course, just talking about the principles frustrates the people at the demand-supply interface even further because they view that as theoretical rather than action oriented.

Yet another way to look at the issue is to think of a repository as a means of supporting policy makers. For example, the ePSI*plus* project has a number of objectives related to policy implementation.

The question then arises: How do you disseminate and implement policies through educational practices and professional development to such a huge number of people? Legislation alone does not help. Politicians may give speeches in support of a law, they may even ratify it to show that they support it, but then they may do absolutely nothing afterwards, committing no resources to its implementation. It is therefore necessary to come in below the political level to help implement it.

The European Union provides an example of having a law—the PSI Directive that the region is trying to implement—that is not coming along as expected. There is a framework defined in a directive, so why is that not working as well as it is intended? What is the real issue? One can promote the directive or the policies, but there is still inertia to overcome.

One of the issues that came up in the Group A discussions is how politicians can be convinced to put resources into these activities, bearing in mind that the politicians are only there for a short interval of time and they are looking for votes. If there are no votes in this, why should politicians decide to put anything into it? One way to convince them is to use multifaceted information channels. Promotion of online discussions on a repository in various forms may be a way to increase political interest in the topic.

One workshop participant thought that there is a great deal of frustration about the pace of change of PSI policy and practice in Europe. This frustration is what triggers the interest in alternative data sets in the private sector. Like any market, if access to data is blocked it encourages the creation of new industries and services to circumvent that blockage. This then raises an interesting economic question: Is the pre-existing information asset in the public sector slowly degrading in value? In some cases the substitute private-sector data sets are now being used by the public sector, and the government is not even using its own data.

Another workshop participant, however, expressed the view that the situation is not as bad in the EU as the previous participant suggested. Much has occurred in various parts of Europe in recent years. For example, Slovenia, which 20 years ago was under a very different regime, today has a commissioner for information who is looking into public information policy issues, such as data protection, access to information, and reuse of information. Many things are happening in various EU member states, and even though much more ought to happen, it is not accurate to give the impression that the situation with regard to PSI policy and practice is not improving.

To take another example, just recently Sweden adopted new PSI legislation, which would not have happened before the EU directive. Indeed, there are several exclusive deals in other countries between government entities and the private sector for providing PSI-related services. How can the PSI practitioners and policy makers in Europe build on these developments? Or, to frame the question differently, how can they build on the successes so that they may get much more economic and social value from PSI based on evidence and solid policies?

This is one reason why it is important to focus on what would happen if the government were to withdraw the public sector information that is now competing with the private sector information. Does one look at what extra benefits the PSI adds, or does one look at what the remainder is if you take it away? A good argument to put to politicians is to say, "These are the sort of things that would happen, and these are the sort of costs if you did not have the PSI in question." One can take that a step further and point out to the public sector organizations that are not making their data available or not making them available at the right price or form that in the long term they are cutting their own throats because in many cases the private sector will find other ways to compete—not always as good, but in some cases better. So public sector bodies ought to take a longer-term view. Given that the technology may have moved on and many of other factors may have changed from when they were first set up to do PSI activities that were considered public tasks at the time, is it still necessary for them to be engaged in these activities? Or would it be better if those functions were left to the private sector, either as some sort of universal service obligation or otherwise?

The classic example is the mapping of remote areas, a task in which the private sector has traditionally had little interest. This may be handled in two ways. Either the government can be tasked with doing the mapping, funded by the taxpayer, or the mapping can be privatized, but either way there has to be a universal service obligation. The private-sector entity would not normally be attracted to performing this type of task without a government contract.

With regard to the role of the private sector in PSI activities in Europe, it is difficult to prove the value of something that does not yet fully exist. One industry association based in the United Kingdom has been collecting case studies from its members. They tend to be quite small scale, but in some cases a big business has been built on PSI licensing terms that would no longer be permitted in the United Kingdom and in the European Union more generally. To look at the value of such activities and to analyze the benefits of the product being offered is an expensive and complex task. To get such case studies, an investment must be made, and there is not yet a large number of them to show to policy-makers.

On the broader question of what the market is going to do, at least some sectors within PSI should be quite dynamic. Already there is very substantial user demand which is expected to grow as devices get more mobile. For instance, as people demand more information of all types, starting with geospatial and weather data, there will be substantial growth, which is why some of the giants in the information sector are entering those markets. The market will bring these PSI-based products and services into the mainstream. The link to user-generated content is yet another factor. The OECD principles and related policy activities regarding PSI need to be communicated as well as possible to these stakeholders.

Another consideration in the three areas of follow-up activities that have been identified here—the manual, the repository, and academic or other kinds of research—is how to promote or contribute to these activities and who the important stakeholders are that should be contacted. One suggestion was that the online repository or platform could include a network of important contacts. Perhaps ePSI*plus* is better placed than OECD to do this in Europe in the near term. Before the ePSI*plus* project is completed, the European Commission may be willing to issue a solicitation for the funding of a repository at some European research institution that would also include information from outside Europe. The ePSI*plus* repository could be added into this new repository, thus preserving the data, providing a start-up base, and avoiding wasteful duplication of effort. To be comprehensive and global, this new repository may require an interlinked network of Web sites.

The EU Committee on Consumer and Competition Policy is another group that could provide an appropriate forum. There is a genuine need to get more research done in this area and to convince the academics and others doing research that this is an interesting topic to pursue. There are many issues here—societal, information processing, government structures, and others—that need to be examined. It would be good to encourage more research, especially by young people.

A recognition or an award scheme could be useful in this regard. There are awards given in the area of *e*-government in Europe and elsewhere in the world already. Perhaps one with several categories could be established in this area to encourage people to do research on PSI. Many researchers have been working hard and getting good results, but they have not received much recognition for their efforts.

Appendixes

APPENDIX A

Meeting Agenda

*The Socioeconomic Effects of Public Sector Information on Digital Networks:
Toward a Better Understanding of Different Access and Reuse Policies*

Organized by:
U.S. National Committee for CODATA
Board on International Scientific Organizations, U.S. National Academy of Sciences
in collaboration with the
Organisation for Economic Co-operation and Development

Place: OECD Headquarters
Conference Centre Room 13
2 rue André-Pascal, Paris 75016, France
Dates: 4-5 February 2008

Agenda

Day one:

9:00   Registration

Session One: **Introduction and opening presentations**

Chair: Daniela Battisti, Agency for Inward Investments and Business Development, Italy, Chair WPIE

10:00	Welcoming remarks and introductions	Graham Vickery, OECD
10:20	Workshop objectives and structure	Paul Uhlir, United States National Academies
10:30	The social and economic goals and values of PSI online: EU government perspective	Jim Wretham, OPSI, United Kingdom
10:50	The social and economic goals and values of PSI online: U.S. government perspective	Nancy Weiss, Institute of Museum and Library Services,

		United States
11:10	The value to industry of PSI: The business sector perspective	Dr. Martin Fornefeld MICUS Management Consulting, Germany
11:30	Achieving fair and open access to PSI for maximum returns	Michael Nicholson, PSI Alliance, United Kingdom
11:50	Open Discussion Moderator: Javier Hernandez-Ros, EC	
12:15	Lunch	

Session Two: **Different approaches for evaluating the direct and indirect economic and non-economic benefits and costs of PSI access and reuse policies in the online environment**

Chair: Antti Eskola, Ministry of Employment and the Economy, Finland

13:50	Public Sector Information: Why bother? Measuring European Public Sector Information Resources	Robbin te Velde, Dialogic, Netherlands
14:10	Measuring the Economic Impact of the PSI Directive in the Context of the 2008 Review	Chris Corbin, ePSI*plus*, United Kingdom
14:30	Different PSI Access Policies and their Impact	Frederika Welle Donker, Delft University of Technology, Netherlands
14:50	The Price of Everything but the Value of Nothing	Antoinette Graves, OFT, United Kingdom
15:10	Enhancing Access to Government Information: Economic Theory as It Applies to Statistics Canada	Kirsti Nilsen, University of Western Ontario, Canada
15:30	Assessing the Impact of Public Sector Geographic Information	Max Craglia, Institute for Environment and Sustainability, JRC, Italy
15:50	Coffee break	
16:40	Assessing the Economic and Social Effects of	Rodney F. Weiher

16:40	Assessing the Economic and Social Effects of NOAA Data Online	Rodney F. Weiher NOAA Chief Economist, United States
17:00	Exploring the Impacts of Enhanced Access to Publicly Funded Research	John Houghton, Victoria University, Australia
17:20	General discussion	

Day two: Morning

Session Three: **Measuring the economic and social costs and benefits of the PSI: Evaluation of the existing approaches and suggestions for future work**
Parallel sessions (a) and (b)

Presenters: Paul F. Uhlir and Raed Sharif
Rapporteurs: Juan Carlos De Martin and Tilman Merz

To facilitate discussion and to advance the analytical agenda, the workshop will be divided into two parallel sessions, with government representatives and PSI supply-side experts in group (a) and industry representatives and users in group (b).

9:00-
12:15

Each session will comprise:
* An overview on different approaches for evaluating the direct and indirect economic and social benefits and costs of access and reuse policies for PSI in the online environment. This will draw on the published literature, the OECD study and on recent analytical work.
* A 90-minute panel discussion addressing questions including:
  1. What are the commonalities and differences among the analytical methods presented in session 2?
  2. What are their main strengths and weaknesses, e.g. their accuracy, comprehensiveness, relevance, validity and reliability?
  3. What are the most effective metrics/indicators to assess particular kinds of information/policies? Are there approaches and metrics/indicators that effectively measure the network effects of the use of PSI online?
  4. What still needs to be known about the application of these methods to the evaluation of public information policies in the online environment?
  5. What theoretical frameworks, models and best practices in other areas can be applied to assess different policies of access to and reuse of digital PSI?
  6. What are some future directions and recommendations for the better study and measurement of access to and reuse of PSI online?
* Following the break, the main points from the panel discussions will be summarized by the rapporteurs (Juan Carlos de Martin and Tilman Merz), followed by discussion. This will be designed to identify activities that could enhance understanding of the economic value and effects of different approaches to access to and reuse of online digital PSI.

9:00-9:10	**Session chair introduction**	

(a) Eivind Lorentzen, Ministry of Trade and Industry, Norway

(b) Jean-Jacques Sahel, Director, Government and Regulatory Affairs, Skype-Europe

9:10-9:30	***Presentation***
9:30-11:00	***Panel discussion***
11:00-11:20	***Coffee break***
11:20-12:15	***General discussion and proposals for future work***
12:15-13:45	***Lunch***

Session Four: Plenary discussion: Wrap-up, conclusions and future work
Chair: Daniela Battisti

13:50-14:10	***Rapporteur presentation Session three (a)***	Juan Carlos de Martin, Turin Polytechnic, Italy
14:10-14:30	***Rapporteur presentation Session three (b)***	Tilman Merz, consultant
14:30-15:50	***Discussion: What do we know and what next?***	
15:50-16:00	***Concluding remarks***	Graham Vickery, OECD
		Paul Uhlir, United States The National Academies

End of meeting

APPENDIX B

Biographical Summaries of Workshop Chairs, Presenters, and Rapporteurs

Daniela G. Battisti (Ph.D., 1994) is a director of the Inward Investments Unit within the National Agency for Inward Investments and Business Development. Since 2004, when she joined the agency, she has successfully launched new projects and managed complex horizontal projects that involve different layers (central and local) of the public administration. Between 2001 and 2004 she was Coordinator of the Research and Study and member of the Board of Technical Advisors in the cabinet of the Minister for Innovation and Technologies. In 1999 she joined the Italian Presidency of the Council of Ministers. Before that she was involved in numerous R&D projects in the field of ICT. She is chair of the WPIE (Working Party on the Information Economy). She is also a member of the Global Advisory Board for the London Business School.

Christopher E.H. Corbin is currently an analyst within the European Union eContent*plus* funded ePSI*plus* Thematic Network, where he has several responsibilities, including: the thematic area of the impact of the EU Directive on public sector information with respect to financial charges made by public sector information holders, coordinating Member State national meetings, providing regular news content to the ePSI*plus* Web site, and maintaining the ePSI*plus* scorecard which ranks EU member states' implementation of the directive.

Juan Carlos De Martin is currently serving as associate professor of information engineering at the Politecnico di Torino, Italy. Dr. De Martin's research activities are focused on multimedia processing and transmission. He spent two years (1993-1995) as visiting scholar at the University of California, Santa Barbara, and two years (1996-1998) in Dallas as a member of the technical staff at Texas Instruments as well as an adjunct professor at the University of Texas (1999). Between 1998 and 2005 he served as a principal researcher at the National Research Council (CNR) of Italy in Torino, where he led the multimedia communications research group. Dr. De Martin is also active in exploring the interaction between digital technologies and society. In this regard, in 2006 he founded the NEXA Center for Internet and Society of the Politecnico di Torino; he is also the coordinator of COMMUNIA, the European thematic network on the digital public domain funded by the European Commission (2007-2010). He is the author or co-author of more than ninety international scientific publications as well as an expert evaluator of research programs for, among others, the Italian Ministry of Industry. Dr. De Martin is a member of IEEE.

Antti Eskola is currently serving as a commercial counselor at the Innovation Department of the Finnish Ministry of Employment and the Economy. His responsibilities include information-society-related innovation policy issues, including the promotion of commercial reuse of public sector information. Mr. Eskola has been active in the OECD Working Party on the Information

Economy drafting work on the Recommendation of the OECD Council for enhanced access and more effective use of public sector information.

Martin Fornefeld is the chief executive officer of MICUS Management Consulting at its Düsseldorf, Germany, location. After his three-year assistant position at the Technical University of Clausthal with foreign studies in Berkeley, California. and Asia, he held a management position at Siemens Nixdorf Informations systeme AG. Subsequently he was director with joint proxy of an international consultancy firm for nine years and finally partner of the firm before he established MICUS Management Consulting jointly with Jutta Lautenschlager in 2000. Dr. Fornefeld is chairman of the IWG-Network, an association of companies and organizations created to increase the economic impact of the reuse of PSI in Germany. Dr. Fornefeld's expertise lies in the areas of strategy consulting, market studies, and public-private business models/partnerships, which he developed substantially in recent years, particularly in the area of public sector information and broadband development in Europe. He earned his Ph.D. in engineering from the University of Clausthal in Germany.

Antoinette Graves led the U.K. Office of Fair Trading's market study on the Commercial Use of Public Information, which was released in December 2006. She participated in the OECD's Working Party on the Information ecEonomy, presented to the European Commission-funded ePSI*plus* conferences, and continued to take an interest in public sector information until she left the OFT in December 2008 to take up a post as a senior policy advisor at the United Kingdom's Intellectual Property Office.

Javier Hernández-Ros is head of the, Access to Information Unit, DG Information Society and Media, at the European Commission. Trained as a civil engineer at the Universidad Politécnica in Madrid, he has a masters degree in business administration from the Instituto de Empresa. After seven years working for engineering companies in Spain, he joined the European Commission in 1986 and was involved in technology transfer and innovation policies, where he set up the European network of innovation relay centres and the Innovating Regions in Europe network. Since June 2002 he has been head of the Access to Information Unit (formerly, Digital Libraries and Public Sector Information). He is currently coordinating the EU Digital libraries initiative and promoting legal initiatives to support the development of the digital content industry, notably the directive for reuse of public sector information. He was also responsible for the e-Content and the Safer Internet programmes for the period 2002-2005.

John Houghton is a professorial fellow at Victoria University's Centre for Strategic Economic Studies (CSES) and director of the centre's Information Technologies and the Information Economy Program. He has had a number of years experience in information technology policy, more general industry policy, and related economic research. He has published and spoken widely on information technology, industry, and science and technology policy issues. His research is at the interface of theory and practice with a strong focus on the policy application of economic and social theory and of leading-edge research in various relevant fields. Consequently, his contribution tends to be in bringing knowledge and research methods to bear on policy issues in an effort to raise the level of policy debate and improve policy outcomes. He has co-authored several chapters in the past years of the OECD publications *Information Technology Outlook* and *Communications Outlook*. He also publishes annual updates on the Australian ICT industry sponsored by the

Australian Computing Society. In 1998, John was awarded a National Australia Day Council, Australia Day Medal for his contribution to industry policy development.

Eivind Lorentzen works for the Department of Research and Innovation, Norwegian Ministry of Trade and Industry.

Tilman Merz is a German-Canadian management consultant with Roland Berger Strategy Consultants in London. He holds an M.P.A. from the London School of Economics and Political Science and an economics degree from the University of St. Gallen, Switzerland. Prior to and during his postgraduate studies, Tilman worked for the Latin America division of the German Development Bank KfW, the Information Economy Group at the OECD (ICCP), focusing on broadband Internet and public sector information policy, as well as for the U.K. Department for International Development (DFID) on issues of legislative strengthening. Tilman's academic interests revolve around developmental and environmental policy with special emphasis on Latin America. In consulting, Tilman focuses on infrastructure, telecoms, the public sector as well as corporate restructuring.

Michael J. L. Nicholson, B.Sc. F.R.I.C.S., is chairman of the Locus Association (an association of private sector PSI reusers in the United Kingdom) and deputy chairman of the PSI Alliance (the equivalent of Locus for the EU). He is founder and chief executive officer of Intelligent Addressing Limited, the company managing the largest and probably most successful of the local government integrated address data management projects in Europe. His previous business, Property Intelligence PLC, was sold to the Costar Group of Bethesda, Maryland, in 2003.

Kirsti Nilsen is an independent researcher and writer. Until her retirement she was a faculty member for a number of years in the Faculty of Information and Media Studies at the University of Western Ontario, and has also taught as an adjunct and visiting professor at other universities in North America and Scandinavia. She is particularly interested in the area of information policy, focusing on public sector information and trade policy. She is the author of *The Impact of Information Policy* (Ablex, 2001), and co-author of *Constraining Public Libraries: The World Trade Organization's General Agreement on Trade in Services* (Scarecrow Press, 2006). A review of the literature on the economics of information prepared under contract for Statistics Canada in 2007 is the basis for the presentation included in this publication. Kirsti Nilsen has also published a book chapter on e-government and another on international trade policy, along with articles and conference proceedings both on various aspects of information policy and in her other areas of interest. She is currently convener of the International Trade Treaties Working Group of the Canadian Library Association, and a past president of the Canadian Association for Information Science. A graduate of Emerson College and Simmons College in Boston, she received her Ph.D. from the University of Toronto.

Jean-Jacques Sahel is director of government and regulatory affairs for Europe at Skype. Previously Mr. Sahel was deputy director of services industries in U.K. Trade and Investment (UKTI), the British Government's external trade promotion arm. There he led the initiative to promote overseas the United Kingdom's strength in financial services. Before that, he held senior posts at the Department of Trade and Industry, among them head of global communications policy. Jean-Jacques served UK interests in many telecoms and IT negotiations and forums during his years in public service. These included the OECD, where he was a vice chair of the anti-spam task force and chairman of the Working Party on the Information Economy (2005-2007); the ITU; the United Nation's World Summit on the Information Society; and the WTO. He is the current U.K. signatory of the 2006 UN ITU treaties.

Raed M. Sharif is a Ph.D. candidate in information science and technology and an adjunct professor at the School of Information Studies at Syracuse University. Raed's research focuses on access to and reuse of public sector information and its impact on scientific and socioeconomic development. He worked for over two years (2005-2007) as a research associate with the Office of International Scientific and Technical Information Programs (ISTIP) at the U.S. National Academies and with the U.S. National Committee on CODATA, where he was involved in designing, launching, and evaluating science and technology policy projects and activities. He is a member of the CODATA task group on Preservation of and Access to Scientific and Technical Data in Developing Countries and a steering committee member at the InterAcademy Panel on International Issues (IAP) Program on Digital Knowledge Resources and Infrastructure in Developing Countries. Raed is also active in promoting the involvement of young scientists in the science and technology policy-making processes. To that end he is currently chairing the Young Scientists Forum at the U.N. Global Alliance for ICT and Development (GAID) Community of Expertise on Enhancing Access to and Application of Scientific Data in Developing Countries (e-SDDC). Before starting his doctoral studies, Raed worked for five years as a business development manager at Birzeit University in Palestine. He also worked as a consultant for the UNESCO, UNDP, EU, and USAID on ICT-related projects and their impact on the Palestinian people and economy. Raed received his bachelors degree in economics and political science in 1999 and his M.B.A. in 2002 from Birzeit University in Palestine.

Robbin te Velde is senior researcher at Dialogic Innovation & Interaction, a small research firm in the Netherlands. He has extensive knowledge in the field of STI policy with a strong focus on IT. He has also worked at technical universities and research consultancies where he conducted many international comparative studies on ICT-related matters on behalf of national and supranational public institutes (covering Europe, North America, Asia, and the Middle East). His background is in administrative sciences, specializing in international relations and economics, and in the philosophy of science. He has written a large number of scientific articles in a wide range of areas such as international politics, philosophy, knowledge management, business administration, technology policy, and information management.

Paul F. Uhlir, J.D., is director of the Board on Research Data and Information, including the U.S. National Committee for CODATA, at the U.S. National Academies in Washington, D.C. His area of emphasis is issues at the interface of science, technology, and law, with a primary focus on digital information policy and management. Prior to that, he worked in the following capacities at the National Academies: director of the Office of International Scientific and Technical Information Programs, 1999-2008; associate executive director of the Commission on Physical Sciences, Mathematics, and Applications, 1991-1999; and senior staff officer at the Space Studies Board, 1985-1991, where he managed projects on solar system exploration and environmental remote sensing programs for NASA. Before joining the National Academies, he worked on remote sensing law and intergovernmental cooperation in meteorological satellite programs at the general counsel's office of the National Oceanic and Atmospheric Administration in the Department of Commerce. He has published and lectured widely and has been involved in numerous consulting and pro bono activities. He holds a B.A in history from the University of Oregon and a J.D. and M.A. in international relations from the University of San Diego.

Graham Vickery is head of the Information Economy Group in the Information, Computer and Communications Policy Division of OECD in Paris. As head of the Information Economy Group and programme director for OECD information technology, he oversees digital content and industry programmes covering e-business, information economy, intangibles and intellectual capital, new technologies, industrial performance, manufacturing flexibility, work organization, and industry globalization. He is the author of numerous OECD publications and articles and has presented papers at many international conferences on the information economy, technology strategies, sector developments, and government policies.

Rodney Weiher is the chief economist of the National Oceanic and Atmospheric Administration (NOAA) in Washington, D.C., where he develops and leads a series of peer-reviewed studies and analyses of the economic dimensions of NOAA's programs, products, and services. These studies include cost-benefit analyses of major earth observing systems, quantitative estimates of the economic benefits of weather, climate, ocean and other forecasts, and valuation of non-market environmental assets. He also advises senior NOAA management on economic issues of relevance to the agency and serves on various interagency and international economic forums. Weiher previously served as a career senior executive to the White House's Office of Management and Budget in the areas of energy, environment, and natural resources, as well as serving in senior positions dealing with energy issues in the private sector. He holds a Ph.D. in economics from the University of Virginia. In the fall of 2008 he retired from federal service and now consults on a variety of economic issues.

Nancy E. Weiss serves as general counsel of the Institute of Museum and Library Services (IMLS), a U.S. government agency that advances museum, library, and information services, and provides financial assistance to the nation's 122,000 libraries and 17,500 museums. In this capacity she provides expert advice on the legal aspects of cultural activity and information policy-making, public/private partnerships, and federal financial assistance, and helps ensure that key policy documents recognize the important role that libraries and museums play in economic development, the creation, dissemination, and preservation of knowledge, and the design and management of the technological infrastructure for the 21st century. Prior to joining IMLS, Nancy served as deputy general counsel of the National Endowment for the Humanities, where she also provided counsel to the U.S. Arts and Artifacts Indemnity Program and represented the agency on the National Archives and Records Administration Trust Fund Board. Nancy earlier practiced litigation and media law at Williams and Connolly in Washington D.C., held a legal research fellowship in New Delhi, India, and completed a federal judicial clerkship with the Hon. William W. Schwarzer (N.D. California and director of the Federal Judicial Center). Nancy graduated with honors from the University of Michigan Law School, and Phi Beta Kappa with a degree in economics from the Wharton School of the University of Pennsylvania.

Frederika M. Welle Donker, M.Sc., works for the OTB Research Institute for Housing, Urban and Mobility Studies, Geo Information and Land Development Section at Delft University of Technology in The Netherlands. After graduating in electronics engineering at North Sydney College of TAFE in Australia, she worked as a technical officer at the Commonwealth Scientific &

Industrial Research Organisation and at the University of Sydney. She completed her M.Sc. with the Faculty of Technology, Policy & Management of Delft University of Technology in 2001. She then worked for three years as a research assistant at the Erasmus Medical Centre (Faculty of Medicine, Erasmus University) in Rotterdam. Since 2005 Frederika has been a researcher at the OTB Research Institute for Housing, Urban and Mobility Studies at Delft University of Technology. Between 2005 and 2008 she has focused on geo portals and the accessibility of geo information, including legal aspects of accessibility and economic aspects such as pricing models. In 2009 she will begin a Ph.D. study titled Impact of the European Union Framework on the Free Flow of Geo Information and Geo Services. Her other research interests are policy development with respect to the role of the public sector in the geo information market and reuse of public sector information to develop value added products and services and Web 2.0 applications in Europe, Australia, the United States, and Canada.

Jim Wretham is head of information policy at the Office of Public Sector Information in the United Kingdom. He has been involved in copyright and information issues for the best part of twenty years. Initially he led a team that managed the licensing of Crown and Parliamentary copyright in Her Majesty's Stationery Office. Following the privatization of the trading functions of HMSO in 1996, he transferred to the Cabinet Office as the head of licensing. Since then his role has taken on a much wider information remit, becoming head of information policy in 2001. In that role Jim was one of the lead officials for the United Kingdom in the negotiation of the European Directive on the Re-use of Public Sector Information. He also played a leading role in the drafting of the U.K. regulations that implemented the directive. As a member of the Office of Public Sector Information, he joined the National Archives in 2006.